I :

A OUT

OF ADISE

According to Bill Murray, in Loch Goil he found "the best bit of country I have yet seen in any part of the world". And this well-travelled writer visited quite a few parts of the world, including the Alps and the Himalayas. As he wrote in the *Scottish Field* in April 1956:

On each return from abroad I find myself dazzled by Scotland. From mid-May to mid-June especially the west Highlands are like a slice out of Paradise. On my last expedition to the Nepali Himalaya I had to leave Loch Goil at the beginning of May. The trees were greening, poppies bursting yellow, flowering-currants and daffodils blossoming full, scarlet rhododendrons breaking the bud, azaleas reddening for the later riot, the cherries shedding a daily rain of spent bloom, and each morning the dawn chorus swelled, and swelled. The loch stretched blue between the hills, still like ice (and as cold); its gentle lap-lap against the rock under the house being interrupted now and then by the equally timeless call of a cuckoo in the orchard. At the thought of leaving all this for Nepal I felt a most unholy goat. When I came back five months later my surmise had been confirmed. Travel as far as I will, I can find many a scene to compare with the Scottish Lowlands, but none at all to match the Highland excellence.

LOCH GOIL:
A SLICE OUT OF PARADISE

Lochgoil Community Council

First published 2001

Second revised and enlarged edition 2004

A Cataloguing in Publication record is available from the British Library
ISBN 0-9540825-1-6

Typeset and printed by Akros Print Ltd

Contents

FOREWORD

It is a great privilege to be asked to write a few words on such a complete work of Loch Goil. The words "a Slice out of Paradise" typify how I personally view many of the wonderful and special parts of Argyll This extremely well-researched work on Loch Goil has captured our eventful history and places and the many colourful characters that have made it so.

I know it will be a reference on this particular slice of paradise for many years to come.

Argyll..

Acknowledgements

This book, compiled in recognition of the new millennium, is the result of the efforts of a number of people. With the arrival of a new century we are made aware that the entire twentieth century is now part of history, and we have attempted in these pages to incorporate the memories of some of the older inhabitants of Lochgoilhead as well as of those who grew up in the village and subsequently moved away. Readers should bear in mind that people's memories of events differ: while we have endeavoured to cross-check our sources, we cannot claim infallibility when it comes to "facts" or dates. Nor do we claim that this is by any means a comprehensive history. We are grateful to those who supplied information or precious old photgraphs: Joan Aitken, Cathy Boyd, Jackie Boyd, Dougie Cameron, Hugh Cameron-White, Douglas and Jean Campbell, Irene Campbell, Ida Craik, Diane Dewar, Mike Dimmer, Mark Evans, Jack and Margaret Forrest, Len Gow, Andy Hammon, Duncan Henderson, Sheena Jack, Bridget Jensen, Ray Leeper, Mike McCloghrie, Calum MacDonald, Agnes MacDougall, Cathy McGillivray, Donald McGregor, Catriona MacInnes, Sadie MacKenzie, Margaret and Frazer MacKenzie, Jean McPhail, Jean Maughan, Tom and Jean Murray, Hugh and John Neilson, Jimmy Paterson, Sue Prescott, Bunty Walker and Nera Wigham. We should also like to acknowledge the help of Eileen Tisdall, who provided material for Chapter 1, and Eleanor Harris and Murdo MacDonald, local studies librarian and archivist respectively of Argyll and Bute Council. However, the book would not have appeared without a grant towards publishing and development costs from the Heritage Lottery Fund, and we are grateful for their generosity.

While we drew on a good deal of early spadework done by our own indefatigable local historian, Derek Prescott, who also supplied many of the photographs, most of the later jogging of memories and committing that information to paper was undertaken by Eileen McCloghrie, and credit is due to both of these for their hard work over several months. The administration behind the scenes was ably masterminded by Leslie Cuthbertson, whose refreshments cheered our many committee meetings, and the task of putting all the pieces into some kind of logical order fell to Caroline Wilson, a relative newcomer to the village who now feels more than ever that she should have settled in this Slice out of Paradise years ago.

Derek Prescott was born in Lancashire, where he followed an engineering apprenticeship with ICI, moved to Gloucestershire in 1966 to study at teacher training college, and then became a PE teacher in Berkshire. In 1973 he moved to Lochgoilhead to take up a post as an outdoor instructor at Fife's Outdoor Centre. From 1979 he spent some time as a jeweller, working with fine silver and gold wire. An interest in photography developed around 1978, and this has now become his full-time occupation. Photographic commissions play an increasing role in his business, but he specialises in audio-visual presentations encompassing the world of nature and the beauty of the land. His work in this field has gained him an associateship of the Royal Photographic Society; his presentations have taken him on tours throughout Britain and the Netherlands. His fascination with local and Scottish history has led to many years of research on the village of Lochgoilhead and of Scottish and Highland culture.

Eileen McCloghrie has lived in Lochgoilhead since her marriage to Mike in 1986. After working for many years in the electronics industry she retired at the young age of fifty with a view to enjoying a quality life-style in this beautiful part of the world. She has achieved her objective, and now indulges herself in various pastimes, including walking their two collie dogs, gardening (the garden is not yet as low-maintenance as she would like), curling, country dancing, reading, learning to read music and play the piano, DIY, trying to improve her golf, and entertaining visiting grandchildren. She hopes to have more time again for all these activities now that this book is published!

Leslie Cuthbertson arrived in Lochgoilhead thirty-one years ago, when he bought the first of his three chalets. Twenty years later he built the first of his three houses here. From this you can conclude that, while restless by nature, his heart lies in Lochgoilhead. Having run the family dairy business in Glasgow for thirty years, he settled here permanently in the early 1990s and ran a Dunoon-based travel agency until July 2001. He is currently employed (unpaid) as a community councillor and secretary of the Golf Club and has various other local unpaid jobs. His wife Avril shares his love of the place, as do his three children, two sons-in-law and two grandchildren, who visit regularly (too often?). This book is his first published work.

Caroline Wilson arrived in Lochgoilhead only in 1995, but feels as if she has been here a lot longer. She was born in London, studied music at university in Bristol and, following a couple of alternative careers, eventually ended up working as an editor for Macmillan Publishers, in both London and New York, on various large encyclopaedias of music. In an attempt to get away after the third encyclopaedia she turned to freelance editorial work and moved to Oxford, but after a few years there she realised that a shorter working week and an office with a view down a loch were required. While modern communication methods mean that she is still pursued by encyclopaedia publishers, early retirement remains a goal, as she and Jack also have a garden that is not yet as low-maintenance as they would wish.

Acknowledgements for the Second Edition

The compilers of the first edition of *A Slice out of Paradise* were surprised and delighted that the entire print run of a thousand copies was sold out within nine months. Encouraged by the obvious demand for the book, we thought that a reprint could incorporate both our small file of corrections and a new chapter on "the war years". As the deadline neared we amassed more and more information and so many new pictures that this enlarged second edition is in many places radically different from the original, and we hope that those who bought the first edition will also enjoy this revised version.

As before, we are very grateful to those who helped us with fresh information and photographs, most especially Dougie Cameron, Hugh Cameron-White, Duncan Henderson and Hugh Neilson, but also Bob Anderson from Canada, Robin and Sandra Carter, Eric Carroll, Mike Dimmer, Caroline Hood, Jack Lavender, Christina Litster, Cathie MacDonald, Murdo MacDonald, John and Sadie MacKenzie, Ann Matheson, Jean Maughan, Mark and Linda Morpurgo, Michael Moss, Gladys M. Shearer, Iain Smart and Bunty Walker. We are indebted to the Trustees of the National Library of Scotland for permission to reproduce the detail from "A map of such part of His Grace the Duke of Argyle's heritable dukedom" (1734) by John Cowley. And, once again, we could not have proceeded with the new edition without a generous grant for the printing costs from the Heritage Lottery Fund.

CHAPTER ONE

Geographic and Pre-History

The Landscape of the Area

The landscape of Lochgoilhead and the Cowal peninsula is a legacy of over 600 million years of geological and glacial processes. The geology of the region is dominated by the Dalradian rocks which are found right across Scotland, running from Peterhead in the north-east down to the Mull of Kintyre in the south-west. During the Dalradian era an ancient sea called the Iapetus Ocean separated Scotland from England. The Scottish landmass lay at the margins of this ocean, with what is now North America forming the mountainous region inland. The Dalradian rocks record 200 million years of events within this ocean. Sediments such as sands, silts and muds brought down from the mountains inland were deposited and over millions of years were lithified into sandstones, siltstones and mudstones. Thus sediments from ancient North American mountains make up the rocks seen around Lochgoilhead.

Around 430 million years ago the Iapetus Ocean began to close and Scotland and England started to drift closer together. Under the intense heat and pressure generated by the moving together of the two landmasses, the ocean sediments were metamorphosed into layers of pale white quartzites, silver-grey mica-schists and grey-green phyillites and slates. These are the rocks that are found throughout the Lochgoilhead area, and they are beautifully exposed along the Hell's Glen road. The final collision of England and Scotland and the disappearance of the Iapetus Ocean caused intense folding and rapid uplift of the rocks, forming alpine-like mountain ranges across much of Scotland. All the rocks in the Lochgoilhead region are heavily folded and contorted, illustrating the immense forces involved during this period of mountain building known as the Caledonian Orogeny. Within the Cowal peninsula the rocks have been deformed into one large fold – the top of the fold running down the peninsula and rocks in the area turned upside down. The suture line between the Scottish and English landmasses is marked by the Highland Boundary Fault, just to the south of Lochgoilhead.

For the next 350 million years Scotland and England remained attached to North America and other oceans came and went over the landmasses, depositing a sequence of rock types. Over these millennia Scotland's rocks and landscape were subject to intense erosion by wind, rain and rivers. Periodically the landscape was shaken by seismic activity and uplifted, the earth's crust heaving and flexing during further collisions. It was these periods of uplift that resulted in the ancient eroded Dalradian rocks remaining as high mountains.

Finally the continents once again began to move apart, and around 55 million years ago the Atlantic Ocean opened up. This was associated with intense volcanic activity, as the igneous rocks found on Arran, Mull and Skye testify.

The Scottish landscape around 26 million years ago is thought to be very similar to that of today, the west being dissected with many closely spaced valleys as a result of ancient well-established drainage patterns. Once the Atlantic Ocean had fully opened up, the scene was set for the waxing and waning of the great ice sheets associated with the last two million years, the Quaternary period. During this period it is thought that the ice sheets came and went at least 50 times. The ice sheets would have covered all of Scotland, eroding masses of bedrock and soil as they scraped and gouged their way across the landscape. The ice would always move along the same easy path, along the ancient river valleys. Thus each successive ice sheet would travel across the landscape, deepening the same valleys each time and producing steep-sided valleys and fjords such as Loch Long and Loch Goil. Occasionally the ice would force a passage through the landscape, seen today as breeches or cols in the mountains. Ice would also have accumulated in the same areas in the uplands, carving steep-sided corries into the mountains – such as seen on the north side of Ben Donich.

The last ice sheet to cover much of Scotland reached its peak 18,000 years ago, and by 13,000 years ago much of Scotland was ice-free. Around 11,000 years ago there was a short period of renewed ice cover known as the Loch Lomond Readvance. This final period of limited ice cover and arctic climate lasted around 1000 years and had a profound effect on much of the Scottish landscape. Areas such as the Mull of Kintyre, which remained ice-free during this period, retain the rounded profile of a landscape once covered in a larger, older ice sheet. However, the rugged mountains around Lochgoilhead, such as those in the Arrochar Alps, and those in much of the north-west of Scotland illustrate how this final period of ice cover reshaped the landscape, further deepening the corries and defining mountain peaks and ridges.

Scotland finally became ice-free around 10,000 years ago – the result c rapid climatic warming – marking the start of the present period, known as the Holocene. The retreating ice gave rise to distinctive features in the landscape, many of which can be seen in the Lochgoilhead region today. The rapid uplift of the land after the ice retreated would have triggered a series of earthquakes, causing rockfalls, fractures and caves in the rock, such as those seen at Uamh Clachan Caber above Lochgoilhead, through Hell's Glen and on the slopes of Ben Donich.

Changes in sea-level during the Holocene were a result of melting ice and the uplift of the land after the retreat of the ice. The highest sea-level was reached around 6500 years ago, when Scotland was almost an island; the Firth of Forth was as far inland as Aberfoyle and the marine Loch Lomond was connected to the Clyde. The unusually wide and flat valley of the River Goil at Pole flats is evidence for this high sea-level; for a time the valley floor would have been covered by the sea and infilled with marine sands.

The retreating, melting ice would have deposited the eroded bedrock material it was carrying. Material dumped at the snouts of the main valley glaciers such as Loch Long and Loch Goil is thought to lie beneath the water at the point where these two lochs meet. Elsewhere material smeared along the valley sides and valley floors has been reworked during thousands of years of erosion and redeposition by rivers. Material from the rivers pouring off the valley sides has been reformed into large aprons of sediment known as alluvial fans, as seen at Ardnahein and Ardgartan.

With increasing warmth at the opening of the Holocene, vegetation began to spread from the south and the west. Shrubby plants such as juniper, willow, birch and rowan began to replace the initial herbaceous vegetation cover. Mixed deciduous woodlands dominated by hazel, oak and elm, with some birch, were well established in the west of Scotland by around 6500 years ago.

The impacts of both man and climate have changed the landscape around Lochgoilhead. Mesolithic peoples would have been present in Scotland from the opening of the Holocene, around 10,000 years ago. The impact of these peoples on the landscape is limited, though there is some evidence for woodland clearance through burning – the clearings possibly being used to attract animals such as deer. The arrival of agriculture around 5000 years ago effectively meant the large-scale clearance of woodland for farming. Evidence from Kintyre suggests that cereal growing was underway by about 5800 years ago. It is thought that the early farmers were well aware of good soils for agriculture and would have, for example, cleared areas of elm forest, as the soil

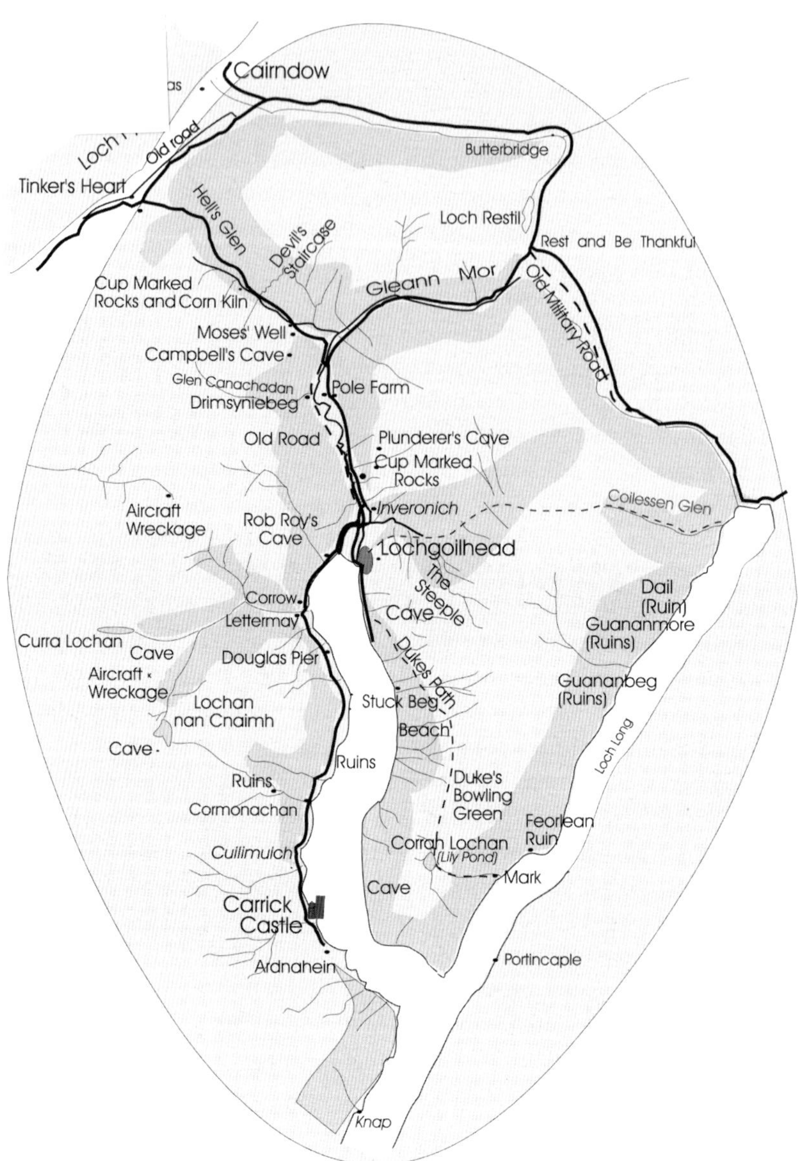

1.1 Local history map of the Loch Goil area

would have been more fertile. The alluvial fans and the valley floors mentioned above are also important sites for early agriculture, in particular within the Loch Goil region, where soils are acid and often of poor quality. Here the constant washing of sediments across the fans and valley floor would ensure that these areas remained fertile. This is borne out by the fact that today many farm buildings are located on these straths or just above the valley floor.

Much of the rugged beauty of this area can be attributed to the initial framing of the land by movements in the earth's crust, followed by the honing down process of immense ice sheets scouring the earth during various Ice Ages. Rises in sea-level and the elevation of the land as the huge weight of the ice was lifted from it further altered the appearance of the landscape, and subsequent erosion by wind, rain and frosts continued the almost imperceptible but incessant shaping. As the ice receded it followed the natural lines of the existing glens, and in so doing enlarged and deepened them, creating the classic U-shaped valleys which are such a feature of the Highlands. This scouring of the glens and the erosion of the mountains and rocks eventually created clay and mud, thus giving the opportunity for plants to become established.

From the warmer, southern climes came a whole host of plant life, and some of the earliest trees would have included birch, hazel, dwarf willow and juniper. The Scots pine, our only native pine, soon became a dominant feature of the Scottish woodlands, with aspen and rowan also becoming well established – although these two fared less well under the shade of the pines. So it was that the Great Wood of Caledon (the Caledonian Pine Forest), eventually covering more than three million acres of the Scottish landscape, became the greatest and most impressive area of primeval pine forest ever in the British Isles. Remnants of the Great Wood can still be seen in the Black Wood of Rannoch, Glen Affric, the Cairngorms and several smaller groupings – as in Glen Cononish between Crianlarich and Tyndrum, just a few miles from Loch Goil.

Within these woods and forests some of the birds and animals we know today would have thrived, and so too would wolves, brown bears, the lynx and other animals, now long since extinct in Britain. The mountains and moors would have supported a rich variety of plant life, much of it similar to the tundra and alpine vegetation now found only in a few isolated locations, such as Ben Lui and Ben Lawers in Perthshire. This, possibly, would still be the scene today if there had been no intervention by the next immigrant to the land – man.

The Arrival of Man

The earliest people to inhabit Scotland were hunters, who would have ventured north in search of new and untapped food supplies. They lived in caves or clearings near the coast, initially just for short periods on seasonal hunting expeditions. Gradually, however, some settlements were established, where an abundance of natural resources would have tempted the normally nomadic people to reject their accustomed lifestyle.

Clearly this did not take place in just a short time. A period of 2000 years or more elapsed before the hunters and gatherers were joined by farmers and true settlements were established. The farmers, too, moved to different locations, but were more inclined to settle in one place for several seasons before moving to new and unworked sites. No doubt an element of trading was introduced, as the hunters exchanged their goods for the grain or other produce of the farmers.

Many cultures thrived throughout Scotland over the centuries, each leaving a wealth of evidence of their presence. Burial chambers and standing stones, many having curious carvings on them, show that each group or culture adapted and modified the cairns and chambers of earlier cultures. There are the remains of a burial cairn above Ardno, about quarter of a mile from the Hell's Glen junction with the main road.

In Hell's Glen, 4 miles from Lochgoilhead, there is further evidence of these early settlers in the area. At the foot of the burn which descends from Cruach nam Mult there is a group of small boulders bearing the indented cup marks left by the people of the Bronze Age. The purpose of cup marks has never been accurately ascertained, but theories ranging from their use as astronomical calculators to their employment to denote the whereabouts of the elements of bronze or other metals have been suggested. The Hell's Glen cup marks are arranged in groups of four in a square formation. Some of the boulders have several groups.

Nearby is a very well-preserved corn kiln, which was used to dry grain – essential to keep it from rotting during storage. Many surviving kilns are in a very poor state of repair or have collapsed entirely, but the Hell's Glen kiln is in remarkably good condition, and with very little repair work could once again be used as it was centuries ago. At the same location there is the remnant of a former crofting site, with two black houses and several outbuildings. A knocking stone used for the grinding of grain can also be seen in a flat slab nearby.

Chapter Two
Early Local History

The Campbells of Ardkinglas

Although the modern parish of Lochgoilhead and Kilmorich unites the villages of Lochgoilhead and Carrick Castle on Loch Goil with Cairndow near the head of Loch Fyne, geographically the two are quite separate. Loch Goil is traditionally associated with Glasgow and the Clyde, whereas Cairndow is more closely linked with Inveraray and Loch Fyne. However, there was a time, extending over six centuries, when Lochgoilhead was a part of the estate of the Campbells of Ardkinglas, centred on Cairndow.

Although the origins of Carrick Castle are a little uncertain, it is well documented from the period when the Campbells took control. The castle came into Campbell jurisdiction around 1334, having previously been a stronghold of the Lamonts. The Lamonts had been a powerful clan in Cowal, being noted since before the untimely death of Alexander III in 1286. They were something of a law unto themselves, holding no allegiance to any king – as was the case with many of the families in Argyll at that time. Being of a line which could possibly be traced back to Somerled of the Isles, they would likely have considered themselves of very high and noble, if not royal, traditions, and perhaps beyond being subject to any sovereign.

John Balliol, the king chosen by the arbitration of Edward I following the death of Alexander, tried to bring the Lamonts to order. This failed, eventually causing a great rift between the MacDonalds (Sir Angus MacDonald was the son of Lamont of Ferchar) and the MacDougals (who were kinfolk of Balliol). It was not until Edward himself had received the fealty of the Lamonts in 1306 that there was anything like peace, albeit temporary, between the rival families.

There were other castles in the area belonging to the Lamonts, including Dunoon Castle, Toward Castle and Ascaig Castle. (The latter two were destroyed in 1646 by Campbell of Ardkinglas and Campbell of Ormsary.)

Ardkinglas

The wife of Sir Neil Campbell of Lochore (Loch Awe) was the sister of Robert the Bruce, and so the Campbells were well established in the royal courts. On an earlier occasion, when William Wallace was encamped near Tyndrum, Sir Neil contacted him from his island castle of Innis Chonnel on Loch Awe. He had arranged to entice a man named MacFadyean, who was known to be a traitor, into the Pass of Brander. Wallace was able to capture the traitor by attacking him from above on the flanks of Ben Cruachan, a ploy used some years later by Robert Bruce himself in defeating the MacDougalls. Sir Neil benefited nicely from this, and was granted the lands around the head of Loch Awe.

Sir Neil's son, Colin Campbell, gained great patronage in accompanying Edward Bruce, Robert's brother, to Ireland in 1316. Further favour was gained by collaborating with Robert Stewart, Robert the Bruce's grandson, in trying to regain control of the West of Scotland from the English in 1334, and he was granted lands throughout Argyll. The ability to be in support of the right people at the right time, and to gain considerable assets from fortuitous marriages, appears to have helped enormously in obtaining both land and power for the Campbells.

Sir Colin was called *Iongantach*, "the Wonderful Colin", and it was one of his sons who was granted the lands of Ardkinglas, including Lochgoilhead and Carrick Castle (the estate also covered Glendaruel, Strachur, Kilmun, Dunoon and Toward). He was known as *Cailean og gharbh chriochan Chomhail*, or "Young Colin of the rough bounds of Cowal", and was the founder of the house of Ardkinglas. Young Colin's son Sir John Campbell had a swarthy complexion, being marked on the face with pitted freckles, and was thus named *Eion Rioch*, "Swarthy John". Some claim that the name *Mhic Eion Rioch*, "Son of Swarthy John", became the patronymic of the Ardkinglas Campbells (*Mac Iain Rhiabhaich*), although Archibald Brown, the author of that most detailed work *The History of Cowal*, disputes this.

The Campbells of Ardkinglas collected rents almost three times the size of those of other families in Argyll, and they were the regulators of all the herring fishing between the Mull of Galloway and the Pentland Firth. They became so powerful that they were often involved with sorting out, and settling, disputes with the awkward neighbours of the house of Argyll.

The Scotland of the 1600s was a very troublesome place. Following the death of Elizabeth I in 1603, with the union of the crowns James VI of

Scotland also became James I of England. His ruling of Scotland was carried out from London, which was none too popular with the Scottish people (some things never change!). Following the battle at Glen Fruin, near Helensburgh, between the MacGregors and the Colquhouns of Luss, James issued orders that the MacGregor name should be banned and that their lands should be confiscated.

2.1 A rather idealised scene at the head of Loch Goil, probably early 19th century

The civil wars later raged throughout Britain, where the parliamentarians fought against what they saw as the tyranny of Charles I. The Scots were divided. The Covenanters, under James Graham (the Marquess of Montrose), were critical of Charles but did not wish to make war on him, while the rich and powerful Archibald Campbell, eighth Earl of Argyll, supported the parliamentarians. In 1644 Montrose and his Jacobites ravaged the Campbell lands of Argyll, defeating Argyll at Inverlochy. The Campbells retaliated against supporters of Montrose and even passive Jacobites. In 1646 the Ardkinglas Campbells burnt Toward Castle and hanged more than 100 Lamonts at Dunoon.

After Charles II died in February 1685 he was succeeded by his brother, James VII, a Roman Catholic. James declared that he would never invade the established government in church or state; however, no sooner did he find himself securely on the throne than he proceeded to act in a despotic manner by causing certain laws to be enacted, in consequence of which a number of the nobility and clergy in both Scotland and England exiled themselves. They took refuge in the Netherlands, where the ninth Earl of Argyll had remained since he had fled in 1681. As the country became disaffected, a double insurrection was planned, to be led in England by the Duke of Monmouth and in Scotland by the Earl of Argyll. Monmouth was defeated, taken prisoner and beheaded. After Argyll had arrived in Scotland he made every effort to raise the clans but could muster only about 2500 men. He was later captured and taken a prisoner to Edinburgh, where he also was beheaded in consequence of the sentence passed on him in 1681.

Following the death of Argyll his estates were plundered by the troops of the Duke of Gordon, the Marquess of Athol and Lord Strathnaver. An account of the depredations was drawn up by an unknown author, probably a son of Mr William Ewing of Bernice, who probably held some part of the adjoining estate of Belzie. From the detail given, it appears to have been compiled with a view to being presented to parliament for a remuneration of the losses sustained, and was probably made about the time the title and estates were restored to the late earl's son, on 1 August 1689. An extract is given below of the affected areas in the Lochgoil region.

***

AN

ACCOUNT

of the

DEPREDATIONS

committed on

THE CLAN CAMPBELL, AND THEIR FOLLOWERS,

IN THE SHIRE OF ARGYLE,

During the Years 1685 *and* 1686,

When the EARL OF ARGYLE rose in Arms to oppose the Tyranny of James VII.

THE LANDS OF GLENCROAW

Item, Robbed and carryed away from ye tennents of
Glencroaw, tuenty-ane horses and mares, thretty-three coues,
tuo hundreth and thretty-nyne sheep and goats,
Some of these were taken away by Duke Gordons men, and
oyrs by my Lord Stranavers, the rest by Lochaber and
Glencoa men.

Item, Their plenishing, and the destruction of yr cornes, and burning of their houses, by the duke of Gordons and Stranavers men, valued at fyve hundreth pounds scots.

THE LANDS OF LITTLE HELLSGLEN

Item, Robbed and taken away from the tennets of Littlehellsglen, tuenty-eight horses and mares, ane hundreth and fourty-three coues, tuo hundreth and seventy-fyve sheep and goats,

Of these, fiftie-three coues were slaughtered in Athols camp. The rest of the coues, sheep and horses were robbed and taken away be Athols forces; except some of them be the duke of Gordons.

Item, Their plenishing, with the destruction of yr cornes, valued at tuo hundreth pounds scots.

THE LANDS OF MEIKLEHELLSGLEN

Item, Robbed and away taken from the tennents of Meiklehellsglen, tuenty-fyve horses and mares, ane hundreth and fourtie-three coues, and ane hundreth and fifty-four sheep,

Item, Taken out of the sds lands, fyve horses, thretty-nyne coues, sextie sheep and goats,

Qrof yr was slaughtered in Athols camp, tuenty-three coues; and the rest carried away be Athols forces, except ane pairt by the duke Gordons.

Item, Yr plenishing, which was robbed and carried away, was valued at tuo hundreth thretty-sex pounds threttein shill. 4d.

THE LANDS OF POLCHORCRAN

Item, Robbed and taken away from the tennents of Polchorchran, tuenty hourses and mares, seventy-ane coues, and nyntie-nyne sheep and goats,

These were generally taken away be my Lord Athols forces.

Item, Yr plenishing, nets, and all yr furnitor for the herring fishing, with the destruction of their cornes, valued at tuo hundreth pounds scots.

THE LANDS OF INNERROUICH
Item, Robbed and away taken from the tennents of Innerouich, threttie horses and mares, sextie coues, and ane hundreth and three sheep,
Of these seventein coues were slaughtered in Athols camp, and all the rest taken away be his forces.
Item, Yr plenishing, with their herring nets, valued at tuo hundreth and sextie-sex pounds, four shill. four pennies, taken away be sds forces.

THE LANDS OF LOCHGOYLSHEAD AND CRAIG
Item, Robbed and taken away from the tennents of Lochgoylshead and Craig, fifty-three mares and horses, eighty coues, and fiftein sheep,
Qrof slaughtered in the marquis of Athols camp, sex coues; and the rest of the horses, coues, and sheep taken away be his forces, and some by duke Gordons and Stranavers.
Item, Their plenishing, with their nets, and many furnitures of their boats, and also some of their boats broken, valued at fyve hundreth pounds scots. All this was by the marquis of Athols forces.

***

The author went on to enumerate the total number of animals taken and state the amount required for each (horses and mares "at 30 lib scots the peice"; cows "at sextein pounds scots"; and sheep and goats "at 40 s. the peice over head") and to calculate the total amount for destroying the "plenishing" – a total for the Ardkinglas estate of £63,630 18s 0d. A similar exercise was carried out for Carrick, where the total came to a more modest £2727 6s 8d.

The Ardkinglas Letter of 1905

The following is a copy of the letter written in 1905 by the curator of Ardkinglas, Niall Diarmid Campbell, later tenth Duke of Argyll, to the tenants at the time when Ardkinglas was sold, after the succession of the Callendars, to Sir Andrew Noble. It describes the line of the Ardkinglas Campbells from the fourteenth century.

To all the native men, vassals and good Tenants dwelling on the lands of Ardkinglass both men and women, greeting:-

Know all you to whom these present letters shall come, or who shall hear them read, that it is neither lightly nor without great grief that We have seen the lands of the ancient Barony of Ardkinglass, through the calamitous and long continued growth of adverse circumstances, pass from the possession of your present Laird, in whose family they have been from the year 1396 to 1906 a period of 640 years. Furthermore for at least a Century before that it can be proved that they were possessed by the Parent House of Lochow or Argyll. A severance of those links of affection forged in the clangorous tumult of those six stormy centuries now lying peacefully behind us is not easy.

Inasmuch as there be few amongst our Native tenants who have not sprung from our Race through far off marriages in the past, when instead of passing to alien lands, it was the wont and pleasant usage of the younger Sons of the Lords of the Soil to settle amongst their own people, and for their sons and their son's sons, and descendants to wed with the daughters of their people, and for their daughters in like manner to marry with the sons of the people, it therefore becomes clear to all men that just in so far as they are sprung from us, so are we from them, and notwithstanding long lapse of ages do but form one vast family, whose interests are one. Wherefore it is not strange that We do bear a greater love for the peoples that remain on those lands, than for those in other districts with which we in the past had less strong ties.

For those of you who have at all studied the question with close attention, it will not be difficult to perceive that in these days the ordinary burdens upon land are so grievous, that when independent sources of support are either slender or totally lacking, it becomes increasingly difficult to hand on an Estate unimpaired to succeeding generations.

More especially is this the case when an Estate is so heavily burdened by an accumulation of debts inherited by its present Possessor from the unwisdom of their forefathers. A point is ever reached in such cases when the interests on money borrowed can no longer be paid, and the lands themselves have to be sold.

This in brief is what has happened not only with the lands We speak to you of, but of nearly all the Lands which march with Ardkinglass. You will all of you recollect that it was but some 10 years ago that the neighbouring Estate of Strachur which (with that of Ardgartan) was held for at least 9 centuries by a Branch of our Race passed into other hands. Drimsynie, Carrick, Ardentinney and Kilmun and even Dunoon all once part of the vast Barony of Ardkinglass and all held by younger Sons of the Parent Stock have long since passed away, with the single exception of Dunoon which is still held by one of the old race.

And though it seem but a span in the lifetime of a planet, and though the hills that keep watch, in their own unchanging silence, over the changing ownership of the Glens, shall smile at the thought, it seems a long time in the History of a Race when we look back at the far off day when Cailein Oig 1st Laird of Ardkinglass with his three tall sons settled, in the place where in obedience to a predicted omen his hamper strings should snap.

But whatever truth or falsity may exist in this particular tradition, we know for certain that his father Sir Colin (Iongatach) Campbell Lord of Lochow did in the year of our Lord 1396 grant to him and his posterity that spot known as Ardkinglass, in feu farm, in all its righteous meaths and marches, with the Patronage of its Churches and Chapels, in all its hawkings, huntings and fowlings etc., and that for "as long as woods should grow and waters run from that year to next year and so on for ever," on condition that he should keep at his own expences two War-Galleys, one of eight oars, the other of six to serve the Lord of Lochow and the King of the Scots in times of tumult and war.

Never was there a more honourable origin for the tenure of land than that which was afforded by the Charters of the Middle Ages, granted from the hands of those Chiefs in Scotland who had already held them for immemorial generations. During all those centuries, it can easily be shewn that the successive holders have continued to be the leaders of their Race in the ever opening and widening fields of action on which the triumphs of an advancing civilisation have been won. For in their strong hands lay vested the only power which in those rough ages could maintain any semblance of civil peace or political order.

It were tedious to relate the life of each of your Old Chiefs on this present occasion, for the tale is a long one and of them far more is known both from Authentic Annals and from fast fading traditions than is usually suspected. Yet a very brief general outline may well find a place herein.

To your first Laird Colin Oig succeeding from son to sire, there has followed a long line of Chieftains of whom your present Laird is the 17th. From Sir lain "Rhiabhaich" Campbell, 2nd Laird all his successors as is known to most of you were called Mac Iain Rhiabhaich and were seldom called anything else by their vassals. So it came about that their individual actions were often confused together.

Sir Colin your 3rd Laird succeeded in about 1460 and died before 1486, and Colin 1st Earl of Argyll became Tutor and Curator to his young Cousin Sir lain the 4th Laird.

It was this Sir lain Campbell who out of a principle of devotion endowed the Chauntry Altar of our Lady, in Lochgoilhead Church in the year 1512, in order that his Mass-priest might there pray for all time to come for the repose of his forefathers, of himself and of his posterity as well as for all the Kings and Queens of Scotland, granting him for that purpose with many other gifts, the pasturage of 8 cows on the lands of Ardkinglass. Was it by some strange foreknowledge or did he little think when he made the pious oblation that only a year and a month were to pass away before his own solemn dirge should be sung at that same altar? For in 1513 he with a great hosting of all his lands joined Archibald 2nd Earl of Argyll and passed with King James IV to the fatal field of Flodden, to fight their old enemies of England. Here fell on the 9th Sept., Argyll, Glenurchy and this Ardkinglass. His reliques were borne homewards by his vassals, with great solemnity and laid with those of his forefathers in the Chauntry Chapel of Lochgoilhead. The bodies of Argyll and Glenurquhy were borne by Dunbarton to Kilmun for burial, because as the old record touchingly has it, "they deyit valiauntlie fechting togidder."

Sir Colin Campbell the 5th Laird was a famous man in his day and to him and Lady Matilda Montgomery his spouse daughter of the Earl of Eglington (and a grand daughter of Colin 1st Earl of Argyll) King James V granted in 1536 what was called the Assize Herring of the Western Seas from the Pentland Firth to the Mull of Galloway including the whole Basin of the Clyde. This Tax was farmed from the Crown by your Ardkinglass Lairds from father to son for centuries and frequently its collection led to sanguinary feuds with the Burgesses of Dunbarton and the Dukes of Lennox, and the Colquhouns of that Ilk.

Sir James the 6th Laird nephew of the last was Historically perhaps the best known of all, for he was Comptroller for many years to King James V. He was Sheriff of Argyll and Tarbut and Chamberlain of Bute, Cowall and Rosneath. Also by the will of Colin 6th Earl of Argyll he was appointed Tutor and Guardian to the youthful Archibald 7th Earl, who was entirely brought up under Sir James' tuition at his Castle of Ardkinglass. So pressing and important did this duty become that the King relieved Ardkinglass of his Comptrollership that he might the better attend on his young Ward, the boy-Earl, but at the same time he was kept for life on the Privy Council by the King's special mandate.

Alexander Campbell his brother in 1566 became Bishop of Brechin. Sir James died in 1591 and his will is extant.

The 7th Earl of Argyll by this will was made Tutor and Guardian of the orphaned children, which post he faithfully filled assisted by Alexander Campbell Bishop of Brechin and Niall Campbell Bishop of Argyll.

Sir lain the 7th Laird succeeded his father. His record is the most ferocious we possess. He murdered the Laird of Calder one of the other Curators of the youthful 7th Earl of Argyll of whom he was violently jealous. He tried to regain the Earl's affections by magical methods summoning all the Witches of Lorne and a Warlock minister called Patrick McQueen for that purpose. The whole of his Trial is extant and

2.2 The sundial, dating from 1626, which commemorates the marriage of Sir Colin Campbell of Ardkinglas; while it is now at the head of the loch, it was probably originally in the grounds of Drimsynie House

2.3, 2.4 *The Renaissance monument, erected in Lochgoilhead Church about 1660, which commemorates James Campbell, 9th Laird of Ardkinglas, whose life was "one long record of tumultuous war, raid and foray"*

shews many a deed of incredible malignity and wickedness. In it is the earliest mention of foot-ball in Scotland that I know of. Though tried on no less than 3 separate occasions owing to the disclosures he made about the complicity of numerous other persons he was never convicted. He met with a strange end by his Galley capsizing off Strone of Glen Siora as he was sailing home from the sacking of the Island of Rathlin in 1615.

Sir Colin the 8th Laird was saved from this Galley by one McDugall of the people of Ardno and yet once again the reigning Earl of Argyll became Tutor to his young kinsman. On the departure of the Earl on an Embassy abroad, Sir Colin was charged with the custody of King's Peace in Cowall in 1618. In 1622 he had a commission from the Privy Council to pursue the

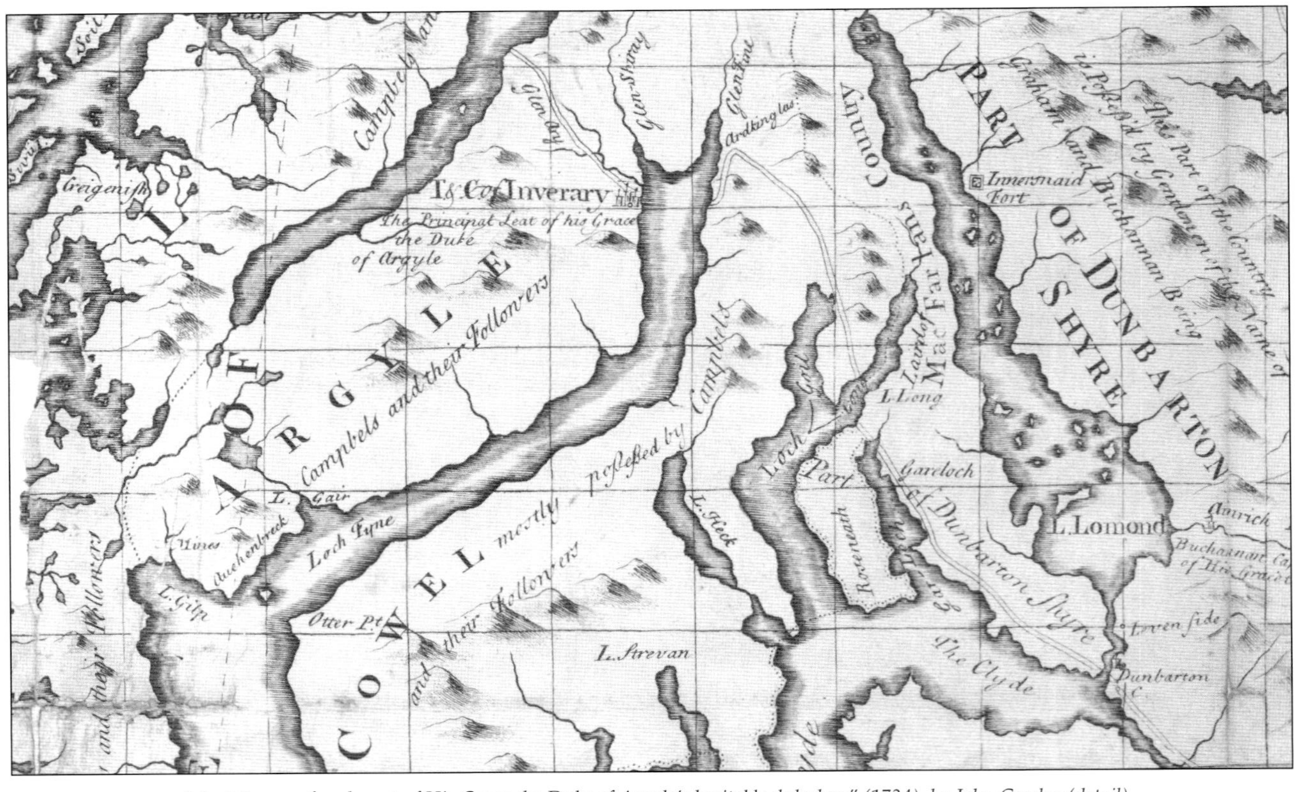

2.5 "A map of such part of His Grace the Duke of Argyle's heritable dukedom" (1734), by John Cowley (detail)

Clan Cameron with fire and sword. In 1625 he is in pursuit of the Clan Ean of Ardnamurchan. He was dead by the year 1643, when his eldest son:–

Sir James 9th Laird whose life is one long record of tumultuous war, raid and foray. In 1645 he was amongst those who escaped from Inverlochy where 40 Campbell lairds lay slain. In 1646 he was defeated at the Battle of Callendar when he had 1200 of his own vassals with him, by the men of Atholl and the Laird of Inchbrakie. In 1654 he was cited before the Privy Council by Sir James Lamont of Inveryne for his murders of many of the latter clan. In 1661 he was indicted for murder by Sir John Lamont of Inveryne and on 3 Sept. 1662 following on his being declared a Fugitive and a traitor, the Lyon King at Arms and his heralds clad in their tubards passed with trumpeters from the Houses of Parliament to the Market Cross of Edinburgh, with the Arms of the traitor Ardkinglass blazoned on paper and affixed them to the Cross backwards and then did rend them in sunder to the sound of trumpets. He was never restored to his honours and barony but his eldest son Sir Colin 10th Laird at the intercession of the 9th Earl of Argyll was fully restored in the year 1665, and was in his father's own lifetime created a Baronet in 1669 by King Charles II by letters under the Great Seal. This is the Laird who hid for more than a year in the romantic cave above Moneveckatan which still bears his name, Uamh-vic-Iain Riabhaich. There he was fed by his faithful tenants when Ardkinglass Castle was in the possession of the Marquis of Atholl, whose followers harried the whole district. In 1684 he was captured and imprisoned first at Blackness Castle and then in 1685 sent on to Edinburgh Castle. He was at last liberated and he became M.P. for Argyll for many years and Sheriff and Justice Depute as well.

After a relentless pursuit for Witches and Warlocks of which he was assured by the Kirk session there was a notable quantity in the Parish, he closed his career in 1709 and his reliques were laid with those of his forefathers in Loch Goilhead Church. His son Sir James the 11th Laird was also M.P. for Argyll and that for the long space of 32 years and he sat in the first Union Parliament. He it was who holding Bonds over the Estate of the MacNachtans of Dundarave obtained finally complete possession of them from Iain McNachtan of that Ilk on the 24 Aug. 1710. Which ancient Clan had held wide lands for at least 800 years and with whom the House of Ardkinglass at one time allied themselves as often in marriage, as they fought with them at another time. In the person of this Laird the direct male line of the House failed, on his death 5 July 1752. It has indeed been asserted that a curse was pronounced by a spey-wife against him, however that may be his 2 sons died young and he devised his Barony to his daughter:-

Helen Campbell who as heiress of Ardkinglass married Sir James Livingstone Bart. who thus became 12th Laird. He lived till 1771 when his son:-

Sir James Livingstone succeeded him as 13th Laird assuming as he did so the name and arms of Campbell of Ardkinglass. He died in 1788 and his son:-

Sir Alexander Campbell Bart. 14th of Ardkinglass succeeded and built a big new house at Ardkinglass. Dying in 1810 he was succeeded by his Cousin:-

James Campbell (formerly Callendar of Craigforth) 15th of Ardkinglass he being the grandson on his mother's side of Helen heiress of Ardkinglass. In his person the Baronetage became extinct although during the whole of his long life he had the inaccurate effrontery to call himself "Sir" to which he as is well proved had no right whatever. He spent nearly all his life abroad owing to his debts which began the great drain on the Estate to which We have already alluded. His life was most varied and interesting for he had visited nearly all the Courts of Europe and he is the only British Subject I feel sure who was present on the great staircase at Versailles when the Paris Mob broke in upon their King Louis XVI and Queen Marie Antoinette and hurried them off to their doom in Paris. He was a witness to all the memorable scenes of that hideous time but these details are given not in his printed Memoirs which are chiefly Military reminiscences but in his private Note Books. In after years he was held as a Prisoner of War by Napoleon, his affairs in Scotland getting into a hopeless confusion. He lived a life of the utmost irregularity yet saw the age of 87 and had 4 lawful wives. His youngest daughter by his 4th wife died only in 1900 and as he was born in 1745 we have two generations spanning the enormous period of 164 years. He died in 1831. His son Col. George Callendar dying during his father's lifetime, he was succeeded in the Estates by his eldest grandson:-

James Henry Callendar 16th of Ardkinglass, who was invested in his lands by his Feudal Chief George 6th Duke of Argyll according to ancient usage in the year 1831, and in August of that same year the House built by Sir Alexander Campbell the 14th Laird was totally destroyed by Fire. Those of you who have reached the necessary span of life will remember this Laird, well enough as well as his wives, he died at Newcastle on 31 Jan. 1851 and his reliques do rest with those of his two wives in the little Church Yard formed by Sir Alexander which yet serves for Kilmorich (Cairndow). All his Callendar ancestors however were buried at Stirling, whilst all his Campbell ancestors were laid to rest at Lochgoil head where two very fine tombs within the Church, one of them as early as the days of the 1st Laird may yet be seen surmounted by 3 despoiled Niches on heraldic brackets.

George Frederick William Callendar his eldest son by Edith Campbell of Islay succeeded him as 17th Laird in the year 1851 and yet once again the reigning Duke of Argyll became Guardian of all the Ardkinglass children, and We could have wished that He might have been your Laird in something more than a name – living amongst you all, to be honoured, reverenced and obeyed in all lawful things as your forefathers did his forefathers in days of yore – and that He might have attained to an old age, hearty and hale surpassing in length of days any of that long line of turbulent ancestors who have passed to Peace or else to yet wider fields of activity behind the Veil.

And inasmuch as this is the last Festival of Yule which shall be celebrated under this old rule and regimen, We, as Curator for George, your Laird, think it but meet and seemly to address you all, in these our letters in this homely and intimate fashion, and to say how much we could have wished to have done for you, and for yours, many things from which circumstances, have prevented us. We doubt little but that your destinies will be as safe, as secure, and as undisturbed in time to come as they have ever been in the past. Such indeed is Our earnest hope and so We do greet you heartily and well until We meet.

Given at Our Messuage of Coombe in Surrey in the Realm of England on the Vigil of Xmass. 1905

Niall Diarmid CAMPBELL
Curator of Arkinglass

It was our intention to have likewise issued these same letters also in the Gaelic Tongue but being anxious for you to receive them speedily this intention has been abandoned.

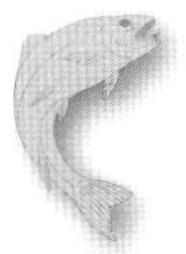

CHAPTER THREE

Statistical Accounts of the 1790s and 1845

These notes and extracts are taken from *The Statistical Accounts*, written by the Revd Mr Dugal McDougal in the 1790s and updated in 1845 by the Revd John McDougal.

Topography and Natural History

The old name of the parish was *Kil nam brathairan – Kil*, from the Gaelic, "signifying a place where a church or chapel was built", and *Brathairan*, "brethren" or "brothers" (the church at Lochgoilhead being "the church of the three brethren") – but from the late 1600s it was generally known as *Lochgoil-head*, meaning a branch of the sea, probably from the Gaelic *gobhal*, meaning "fork". It has also been known as Kinlochgoil or Kinlochgyle – Head of Loch Goil.

The old parish was much more extensive than at present. It included Loch Goil and Carrick, Kilmaglass (now Strachur) and Kilmorich (Cairndow) and extended down Glen Croe to Ardgartan. It was very difficult for parish ministers to perform their duties in such dispersed communities, as was frequently the case in such places as Argyll. To rectify this problem an Act of Parliament was passed in 1649 enabling larger parishes to be divided up and new parishes established. Thus Strachur, Kilmorich and Lochgoil became independent of one another.

The parish was summarised as being about 35 miles long, and from 6 to 20 miles broad, though its shape was too difficult to describe because of the complexity of the outline:

> *as it is intersected by three arms of the sea, divided by mountains, and indented by creeks and promontories. The east part of it is situated on the westward of Lochlong, an arm of the sea, which strikes off from the Firth of Clyde, at first in a north, and afterwards in a north-east direction, and separates the counties of Argyle and Dumbarton. It is about 24 miles in length; but the parish of*

3.1 An early view of the pier at Lochgoilhead

Lochgoil-head occupies no more than 12 miles of its coast. Lochgoil is a small arm of the sea, which strikes off from Lochlong in a north-west direction, and intersects the south division of the parish for six miles. The north-west part of the parish is divided in the same manner by Lochfine. Upon the west side of Lochlong, and upon both sides of Lochgoil, the coast is bold and steep, and the hills high and craggy. The shore, upon both sides of Lochfine, as far as this parish extends, is more flat and accessible; the land is very high, but not so rocky or steep. The barrenness of the ground along the coasts of Lochgoil and Lochlong is partly concealed, and the tremendous wildness of the scene agreeably diversified by extensive natural woods, which cover the land near the coast, and rise to a considerable distance from the shore. The surface of the country in general is very unequal; some of the mountains which form the western extremity of the Grampian hills are situated in this parish. Particularly Bein una [Ben Ime], so called from the richness of its grass; Bein-an-lochan, from the fresh water lake which washes its base; Bein luibhain, abounding in herbs; Bein thiolaire, remarkable for its springs and water-cresses; and Bein Donich, called after a saint of that name. These, and some other hills in this parish, rise to a great height. Some of these mountains are interspersed with huge rocks, caverns, and frightful precipices; in others scarce a rock is to be seen. Till of late they were covered with black heath; but, since they have been chiefly pastured with sheep, they begin to exhibit the pleasing appearance of verdure; and some of them are already green to the very tops. The low lands and valleys form a delightful variety in the surface of this parish.

A description of the soil in the hills implied that it was thin, dry and firm to the tread of cattle, though the higher ground on the hills was wet and spongy, and in some places abounded with deep moss.

For those who know the area well, the following description of the climate will be most appreciated:

The face of the Heavens is generally louring and cloudy; a serene sky is seldom to be seen. The tops of the mountains are most frequently covered with clouds, and, during winter, with snow. The rain is heavy and frequent. The winds, prevented from a free circulation, rush through the glens with irresistible violence; and, at the bottom of high hills and in narrow valleys, the transitions of heat and cold are sudden and excessive.

Despite the weather, the Revd McDougal states in the 1794 statistical account that the local people enjoyed good health. Shepherds were kept fit by their constant exercise and the sea air helped in keeping the fishermen healthy. The most common complaint was that of rheumatism on account of the damp climate and constant changes in the weather. There were, however, 16 people over the age of 80 years, four being above 90 years of age.

The hills around Loch Goil have many caves and deep fissures in the rocks, and in the statistical accounts there are very precise descriptions, particularly for the two most interesting of them – the Campbells' Cave, *Uamh mhic Sion Reoich* ("the son of swarthy John", which is the patronymic name of the Campbells of Ardkinglas), and the Plunderer's Cave, *Uamh na plundarain*. The Campbells' Cave is at the foot of a high cliff behind the large overhanging rock which can been seen above Moses' Well in Hell's Glen, while the Plunderer's Cave is difficult to find. It is hidden in the forested hillside above the forest road entrance a mile below Pole farm.

There are in the parish a great number of natural caves, vaults, and grottos, of different forms and dimensions. One of these caves is situated a little below a very high and tremendous rock, from which a great number of smaller rocks seem to have been torn by some convulsion. Among these smaller rocks is the cave already mentioned. The entry to it is in the form of an arch, about 4 feet high and 3 broad. The cave itself is very spacious, of a circular figure, but not perfectly regular. It is more than 70 feet in circumference, and about 10 feet in height. All around the cave there are smaller vaults, resembling cellars; and, from one part of it, a narrow passage leads to a small apartment, not unlike a sleeping chamber. The cave is covered above by a great number of large rocks, which appear to have been thrown upon one another without any order or regularity; within, it is perfectly dry, but rather dark, having no light but what it receives through the passage already mentioned. This cave is remarkable for having been the sanctuary of one of the lairds of Ardkinglass; who, according to the tradition of the country, having been defeated and oppressed by some powerful neighbour, was obliged to conceal himself, and a few followers, in this cave for a whole year; during which time his vassals and tenants found means to supply him with provisions so secretly, that his retreat was not discovered by the enemy. It is called from this incident, Uamh mhei Sain Reoich. But the most remarkable of all the numerous caves in this country is one which is called Uamh na plundarain. In the face of a steep hill there is a small area between two rocks. At the bottom of this area is a small opening, the mouth of which is covered and concealed from the eye by thick heath and ferns. This narrow and troublesome passage, through which a person of an ordinary size is with great difficulty able to creep, is about 6 feet long, and leads to a small subterraneous apartment, about 10 feet long, 6 broad, and 8 high. Four feet above the bottom of this cave is a small opening, between two rocks, which must be ascended by a ladder, and which leads to a second apartment, about 15 feet long, 12 feet high, and of an irregular breadth. From this there is a narrow and rugged passage to a third apartment, which is also dark. This place is about 24 feet in length, 15 in breadth, and as many in height. The rocks all around are covered with petrified water. The bottom, which is also rock, is perfectly dry. Two large rocks meeting, cover it above, exactly like the roof of a house. Beyond this there is another dark cave, nearly of the same dimensions with the first. These, and a great many other subterraneous apartments in this parish were, in former times, often the residence of a banditti who committed depredations on the neighbourhood. They were also of great service in preserving the persons and the property of the inhabitants, during the deadly feuds and predatory wars which prevailed of old in this country. A few years before the Revolution, the powerful families of Argyle and Athol were attached to opposite parties in the state; in consequence of this, and prompted to revenge by the memory of former injuries, the vassals of the latter made an irruption into Argyleshire. Upon that occasion, the inhabitants of this parish retreated, with their wives, their children, and the most valuable part of their portable effects, to their caves, their strong-holds, and hiding-places, from whence they surprised the enemy in several successful sallies, but could not prevent them from burning many houses, nor from carrying away and destroying much cattle.

Antiquities

At the time these accounts were written the present Ardkinglas House had not been built. On the site was Ardkinglas Castle, which had stood for centuries. The original date of construction is uncertain, but there is evidence of repair work being carried out in 1586. Dunderave Castle (Dunduramh, "the fort of the two oars") is also in the parish. It was a MacNaughton stronghold built around 1596.

Carrick Castle is described as of great strength, and as being built on a rock which was formerly surrounded by the sea:

This castle is built upon a rock, which was formerly surrounded by the sea by means of a deep ditch. The entry to the castle from the land was by a drawbridge, which was defended by a strong wall and two small towers. The castle itself is of an oblong figure, but not perfectly regular, as the architects in laying the foundation kept in some places by the very edge of the rock; it is 66 feet long and 38 feet broad over the walls; the side-wall is 64 feet high and 7 feet thick. Between the castle and the sea there is a part of the rock unoccupied, which was surrounded by a high and strong wall built round the edge of the rock. Within this space 100 men might conveniently stand, for the defence of the castle, if it was attacked by sea. Before the invention of gunpowder, the castle of Carrick could only be taken by surprise; it was scarcely possible to storm it; nor could it be taken by blockade, as it had always a free communication with the sea, for a vessel of any burden will swim along the side of the rock. The time in which this castle was built does not seem to be ascertained. It can be traced up as far as the end of the fifteenth century, but it is probably much older. The tradition of the country is that it was built by the Danes. It was a king's house, and the Duke of Argyle is heritable keeper of it. It was burned by the Athol men.

Quarries

There were several quarries in the area including limestone, but it was found to be cheaper to import limestone from Ireland. A lead mine near the head of Loch Fyne was investigated by a mining company and was found to have quite high levels of silver in the ore, but it was not worked.

Woodland

The area had been heavily wooded at some previous time, but much of the timber was now gone. Excessive clearance of woodland had denuded the landscape during the preparation of land for pasture and ploughing. As a result the value of the remaining wood increased and then became a marketable commodity. The woods in the area were coppiced and managed for the revenue from the timber worth around £500 per year, a sum more than twice that which the land would have generated should the trees have been cleared.

Oak, ash, alder, hazel and birch would have dominated – particularly oak. This, of course, was before the advent of the commercial pine woods of the twentieth century.

Agriculture

Before the time of the first statistical account the land around the parish was much more cultivated. Grain in greater quantities than in the 1790s was produced, with the people more likely to till and plough the land. Even in the 1790s the old Scots plough, which required two men and up to four horses to operate efficiently, was still in use. Some of the more adventurous began to adopt the much lighter and more manageable English plough, which could be operated by just one man and two horses.

Although the area was really unsuitable for ploughing and the growing of crops, there was cultivation up on some of the hillsides, with grain and apotatoes produced. Evidence of this cultivation can still be found today: if the low evening sun glances across the furrows, the signs of old lazy beds are still just visible on the hillsides.

The growing of crops, either grain or potatoes, was often severely inhibited by bad weather, and those grain crops which did mature were of poor yield and quality. Potatoes seemed to produce better yields. Hay was harvested from the end of July through to October, dependent on the weather.

Black Cattle

The district is much better suited to the running of sheep than the black cattle which had dominated for some time before. There were around 2000 black cattle established here by the mid-1790s. (At the same time there were also just under 200 horses in the area.) The dangerous rocks and cliffs in the vicinity proved to be a great hazard for the lumbering black cattle, with as many as a quarter of them not surviving either the harsh terrain or the poor winter feeding in bad crop seasons. The cattle were not of such a large type as those in other areas, but they were well developed and fetched good prices at the trysts (markets) at Crieff and Falkirk.

3.2 Harvesting at Minister's Glebe

These were the same trysts which a few years earlier would have been frequented by that most famous of cattle dealers – Rob Roy MacGregor, whose lands at Craigroyston were just a few miles from Loch Goil on Loch Lomond side. Indeed, it is documented that he used Lochgoilhead as a place to reset some of his more dubious dealings with cattle he had lifted, and having lived in Glen Shira by Inveraray for some years, it is not unlikely that he would have been well known here. He died in 1734, at that time living in Balquhidder in the Trossachs.

The Coming of Sheep

By the 1760s an Ayrshire farmer, John Campbell, had begun to stock this area with sheep. He was followed soon after by more of his countrymen from Ayrshire. They introduced two types of sheep, one a cross between long-tailed white-faced sheep and short-tailed black-faced sheep. The local people were none too welcoming towards these incomers, but they soon began to realise that the sheep were a much more viable means of support. By the 1790s they had adapted to the presence of the animals, and as many as 26,500 sheep were accounted for in the parish.

To prevent a degeneration of the breeding stock, rams were changed every two or three years and ewes were moved on after six years at the most. Gathering took place at least four times a year, firstly for marking, usually in May, and secondly for clipping, in June or July. By August a third gathering took place for the weaning off of lambs, and the final gathering was to separate the rams from the ewes, usually in October. Some sheep were sold directly to butchers in Glasgow, Greenock and Paisley, and if there was a demand then additional gatherings were necessary.

3.3 Shearing sheep at Coilessan, early 1900s

The sheep were smeared to help prevent scab and to protect them from the ravages of the snow and frosts of the winter. If the snow gathered on the backs of the sheep and then froze, they were less able to forage for food because of the additional weight of the snow.

Another problem was a disease called "braxy", which was an inflammation of the bowels and could kill the sheep in just a few hours. The meat from such an animal was considered to be edible if the corpse was found within a day of death, and was eaten either by the servants or cottagers, with some being salted and sent to market. Up to a quarter of the stock could be lost by the disease.

The sheep yielded more wool than those of earlier times, but was of a poorer quality. Fifteen fleeces would weigh one stone, and the output for the area was around 3000 stone per year. Most of this was sent to the woollen factories between Glasgow and Dumbarton. The markets for wool made no discrimination between good and bad fleeces from individual farms. This did nothing to encourage attempts to improve quality in the stock, and it was hoped that the buyers would become more discriminating.

The amount of land required for one man and his sheep would previously have supported up to fourteen tenants. Without doubt the advent of sheep drastically reduced the population of the glens.

Fishing

Fish of a wide variety abounded in Loch Goil, Loch Long and Loch Fyne, with a plentiful supply of whiting, haddock, mackerel and cod being caught. Up to 120 boats sometimes operated in Loch Goil and Loch Long on occasions, occupying 500 men in their search for herring. Loch Fyne, of course, was better known for its herring fishing. Trout and salmon passing through to the rivers were also caught, and in each of two successive years around the 1790s a large sail-fish was caught, one of which was 28 feet long; from it was extracted 150 gallons of oil. On one rare occasion a swordfish 9 feet long, with a 3 foot long "sword", was caught in Loch Long.

Many fish were caught by hand lines, long lines or nets, including flounders and skate. However, the potential of the fishing was not realised properly until men from Nairn, bringing white line (i.e., deep-sea) fishing, came to the area. Locals then understood this potential and began to seize the bounty of the waters for themselves.

Loch Goil and Loch Long had the distinct advantage of being readily accessible for Greenock and Glasgow, and the fish caught in these lochs could

3.4 Fishing for salmon with nets in the loch near the mouth of the River Goil, early 1900s

be transported to the towns very easily. Fish from Loch Fyne, however, had to be carried across Hell's Glen in creels on horseback to the head of Loch Goil before it was shipped, with the disadvantage of additional costs and possible damage to the fish caused by excessive handling. A further advantage for Loch Goil and Loch Long was that they were relatively sheltered from bad weather or storms, thus enabling fishermen to operate when Loch Fyne and open sea fishing was perhaps not as viable.

Wildlife

The wildlife at the end of the eighteenth century was similar to that which is common today, although several species which were around then are now rare or never seen.

Birds such as swallows, cuckoos, fieldfares and woodcock can still be seen, as can such water birds as herons, eider ducks and gulls, but certain species are now much less common. In the account given in 1790s there was reference to dotterel, green and grey phalarope, ptarmigan, grouse and quail. The eagles, too, were "of prodigious size, and remarkable for their strength and ferocity", and were reported as causing great havoc among sheep and young lambs.

Interestingly it was stated that the red deer, which had once been native in the area, was then no longer to be seen. There are, of course, many red deer in the forests and on the hills nowadays.

Foxes, too, were in decline at the time, although this was attributed to the presence of the local fox-hunters, who were appointed jointly by two or three parishes, depending upon the extent of the parishes. The fox-hunter and his dogs were supported by the people: he received a fixed salary and was accommodated by the local tacksman or tenant for a number of nights in the year, dependent upon how much land he possessed. The wildcat was also more common, although the hunter would have pursued these as well. Its habitat in rocky crevices and holes would have made it more difficult to approach.

Population

A survey of the parish, completed on 24 March 1791, revealed the population to be 1012. This figure remained fairly static through the censuses of the first half of the nineteenth century, reaching its maximum in 1831:

1801	1145
1811	1072
1821	1130
1831	1196
1841	1018

However, through the rest of the century the population remained in three figures and reached a low point in 1901.

1851	834
1861	702
1871	766
1881	870
1891	787
1901	671

Chapter Four

Eighteenth- and Nineteenth-Century People and Connections

Donald Ban McArthur

Donald Ban McArthur was born at Drimsyniebeg in the latter half of the 1700s. When he was quite young he moved to Strachur, where he was eventually put to the shoemaking trade. He followed this trade during the winter months and took to fishing during the summer.

At one time he was sent to Glasgow to collect his sister, who, it appeared, had become converted by the preaching of a Gaelic minister. Her employers, thinking that her fanaticism was a sign of becoming deranged, had requested that she be taken home, and the task was allocated to Donald. On the return journey he too was converted and gave up his previously wild and jovial habits. He eventually became a powerful and vociferous orator and preacher, and soon gathered a following of supporters. This, needless to say, upset the established church ministers, who made strong moves to banish Donald and his preaching. They pressed the landowners to ban his ministry on their estates, which Donald and his followers evaded by holding meetings between the high- and low-water marks.

In 1805 Donald was accosted by Colonel Campbell of Southall at Colintraive and transported to Greenock, where he was handed over to a Captain Tatham and pressed into the navy. Eventually his followers traced him to Liverpool. They discovered that his plight was already in the process of being resolved by the intervention of the well-known preachers the Haldane brothers, who had heard of his troubles. Soon afterwards he was released with a certificate from the Admiralty that he should never again be "impressed". He returned to his preaching and continued his ministry. In 1808 he took legal proceedings against Colonel Campbell and was granted the sum of £105 sterling as compensation. Later he became a Baptist and attempted to introduce new followers to the rites of baptism (Loch Eck is supposed to be one of the places where his conversions were made). He fell into disrepute over his interpretation of the Sabbath, and in 1812 he and his young family sailed off to America, where he became a successful farmer in Pennsylvania.

***

RECEPTION OF MR. AND MRS. CALLENDAR OF CRAIGFORTH AND ARDKINLASS

at LOCHGOILHEAD

(newspaper report, 1847)

Monday last was a day of great bustle and excitement at this usually quiet, sequestered, and picturesque watering-place. It was known that Mr. Callendar, the proprietor, and his young and amiable bride, were to come there by special steamer, about four o'clock that afternoon, en route to Ardkinlass Lodge; and the highly respectable body of tenants on the estate of Ardkinlass resolved to give them a Highland welcome on their arrival, in testimony of their attachment to Mr. Callendar as their landlord, and their joy on his marriage with a lady allied to the distinguished families of Islay and Argyll. Accordingly, at earliest dawn, preparations for their reception commenced, which were all completed with astonishing rapidity. Flags were displayed on the neighbouring eminences, as well as at Drimsynie house, the manse, school-house, &c.; a splendid triumphal arch of evergreens and flowers was erected at the head of the quay, and the "Dunniquech Guns" were driven in, attended by the Duke of Argyll's gunners, and placed with another gun in a commanding position to do honour to the occasion. In the course of the day, parties of the tenants, with their servants and others, all in full highland costume, and accompanied by their families, began to arrive, and, added to the resident population and numerous summer visitors, gave promise of an unwonted gathering. As the hour of the expected arrival approached, the scene was truly imposing. The day was beautiful throughout. A body of from fifty to sixty stalwart Highlanders (several of them wearing the tartan of their respective clans) stood lining each side of the road from the arch to the carriage waiting to convey the newly married pair to their destination. The rising ground adjoining was crowded with well-dressed persons of both sexes; the outgoing steamer, full of passengers, lay to off the quay; the flags waved gaily in the wind; and ever and anon the spirit-stirring strains of the bagpipe were falling on the ear. At length it was announced that the steamer was

4.1 A postcard of Lochgoilhead "specially published for Mrs Haggart" of the village post office

in sight, coming up Lochgoil, when the guns commenced firing a salute, which was concluded just as she arrived at the quay. Mr. and Mrs. Callendar were received, on landing, by Mr. Wilson, factor on the Ardkinlass estate, and the Revd J. McDougall, minister of Lochgoilhead, and conducted to the arch, when Mr. McCallum, Ardno, as the oldest tenant on the estate, in a short and suitable address, conveyed to them the congratulations of the tenants and all others present on their auspicious union, and their heartfelt wishes for their long life, health, and happiness. Mr. Callendar having made a most feeling and appropriate reply, he and his lady, whose bland and graceful deportment won the hearts of the whole assemblage, walked between the lines of Celts to their carriage courteously acknowledging their salutations, the way being strewed with flowers by the Misses Woolfield and other young ladies. The Highlanders then took their station in front as a body guard preceded by their pipers, while the other persons connected with the estate followed the carriage; and in this order the cortege passed through the village to the Bridge of Donich, when the Highlanders, opening out on each side, the carriage proceeded a dashing race amidst the enthusiastic cheers of the escort, and the animating sounds of the pibroch. In the evening a large party of the tenants and their friends sat down to an excellent dinner in Macfarlan's Inn

– William Wilson, Esq., occupied the chair, supported by the Revd Mr. McDougall and Samuel Woolfield, Esq., Lochgoilhead. Hugh Macfarlan, Esq., Coilessan, was croupier, supported by Archibald Macfarlan, Esq., Clachan, and Alex. McArthur, Esq., Achadunan. In the course of the proceedings the health of Mr. and Mrs. Callendar was of course drunk with enthusiasm, and a poetical piece, appropriate to the occasion, by Mr. Macgregor, schoolmaster, Lochgoilhead, was read to the company, and loudly applauded. The working people of the neighbourhood were also liberally supplied with refreshments. At a later hour, there was a ball in Mr. Jenkin's new house (obligingly thrown open, and most tastefully decorated with flowers for the occasion), and dancing was kept up to the alternate music of bagpipe and fiddle, with great spirit, till the morning was far advanced, when all departed with the best assurance of having spent a day, and witnessed a scene, to be for ever remembered with gratification and delight.

(The marriage was at St Paul's Church, York Place, Edinburgh)

***

Sarah Munro and Helen Campbell

In the early nineteenth century poor relief was the responsibility of the churches. However, because Calvinists found it difficult to reconcile the ethic of hard work with unemployment, church leaders frequently considered unemployment to be a result of moral failings, and those out of work received nothing. Only the destitute qualified, and even they had to rely largely on private charity. When inspectors of the poor were established in the middle of the century the poor rolls were organised by parish, and evidently the inspectors were keen to disqualify as many applicants as possible. The following letter, dated 17 April 1852, was sent by John Robertson, inspector at Inveraray, to Mr McGregor, inspector at Lochgoilhead:

Case of Sarah Munro

Sir

In answer to your letter of date 31st March last regarding the above case I have to state that I deny the whole statement as incorrect. You say she served with the late Mr McKellar in 1844–45. Mr McKellar died in 1837. You also stated that Sarah Munro was with the late Mr Peter Campbell, provost, from Martinmas 1840 to Whitsunday 1844. The late Mr Peter Campbell died in 1841. The case is yours not ours.

Yours etc.

The same John Robertson, having possibly scored a victory with the above response, wrote again to the inspector at Lochgoilhead, a Mr Smith, on 4 January 1862:

Case of Helen Campbell or Burns. Two children

Sir

The above-named person was sent to jail here for an assault committed on Mrs Ferguson, Artno [Ardno]. *The two children is left with me to be supported until their mother is discharged from prison, the mother being apprehended at Artno your parish is liable for all expenses in this case. Your early admittance will oblidge.*

Yours Respectfully

However, either Mr Smith declined to take on the case or Mr Robertson was covering all angles, as two days later he sent the following letter to the inspector of the poor in Barony parish, Glasgow:

Sir

The above-named person was sent to jail for an assault committed in the parish of Lochgoilhead. Her two children aged about 4 & 7 years was left with me to be supported until their mother was discharged. The children's board amounts to 29/- in all. The mother states she was born in Calton Barony Parish, Glasgow, that she was the wife of Edward Burns, an Irishman, a native of Derry, that she had been married 12 years, that she had seperated from her husband. The husband haveing no resedential settlement, claim is made on the parish of the mother's birth. Your early admission will oblige.

William Barclay

William Barclay is probably best known for his Daily Study Bible, which has been sold in millions in several different countries throughout the world. A deeply religious man, he was called to the ministry and served the church throughout his life. His Lochgoilhead connection is historic. His great-grandparents met and married in the village and lived in Drimsynie House, which they shared with two other families. His grandfather was born in 1823, and a great-uncle, Joseph, was born seven years later. The family worshipped in the church, where they adopted the strong evangelical and Calvinistic values that became their way of life.

The family left two memorials in the village. The first was the Barclay Pier, commonly known as the "Coal Jetty", of which all that remains is a pile of boulders opposite the middle entrance to the chalet site. In its former glory it was an L-shaped structure of considerable size which allowed ocean-going ships to moor alongside, to unload fish and coal. The second, more lasting, memorial is the family's gravestone in the church, which bears reference to the sadness the family must have endured. The deaths are recorded of children aged 10 months, 5 years and 13 years and a young man of 22 years of age.

4.2 Drimsynie House, showing something of the formal gardens

William Leiper and The Lodge

The Glasgow architect William Leiper is best known as the designer of Templeton's carpet factory at Glasgow Green, which is in the Venetian style. Other buildings by him in the city are in Scots baronial, François I and Grecian styles. In the late 1860s he transformed The Lodge, a modest bungalow built on Loch Goil in 1862, into a villa in a Swiss-American-Japanese style for Alexander and Jane Fergusson, who had been given the small summer residence in payment of a bad debt. Another storey was added, as well as a first-floor veranda and a back extension, and Leiper also worked on the rest of the estate, adding a gardener's cottage, stables, a boat house and a summer house and landscaping the gardens. The finest room is probably the drawing room, which has a huge inglenook fireplace and pre-Raphaelite stained glass pieces incorporating the initials of the original owners. Alexander Fergusson, a merchant in Glasgow, died in 1901 and is buried in Lochgoilhead churchyard. His descendants, the Forman family, lived in the house from 1924 to 1954, during which time it was again extended.

Jane Fergusson (1837–1920), the wife of Alexander Fergusson (1825–1901), seems to have been a dominant presence at The Lodge. The following was written by one of her granddaughters, R. G. Leeds, in 1956:

> *Some time in the 1860s our grandfather acquired a small house on the western shore of Loch Goil and it became the beloved summer and holiday resort, not only of his own family but of an enormous number of relations and friends, and warm-hearted hospitality was extended to all and sundry. The Lodge, as it was called, was added to through the years as the grandchildren increased in numbers, and never had children a more wonderful holiday home. The families had to take turns in coming as – elastic though the house was – all the grandchildren, accompanied by parents, nurses and governesses, could not be accommodated at once, but there was one halcyon summer when Tennants (two families), Leeds and Crewdsons filled three houses, and boating, bathing, fishing, paddling, picnics, and wild games of red indians in the woods took place.*
>
> *When staying with Grandmother she made few rules for our behaviour, but in whatever barefooted state we had run about all morning, shoes and stockings had to be resumed for lunch, and afterwards we girls were expected to sit quietly for half an hour in the drawing-room with some needlework or other peaceful occupation. When the sound of the paddles of the steamer from Glasgow was heard before lunch Gran would watch its arrival at the pier, about half a mile away, through a telescope which stood on the verandah, and if she spied any relations or friends disembarking would exclaim,*

"There is cousin E___, or Aunt S___, or Dr D___", and would ring to have extra places set at the table; no unannounced incursion ever put her out, and there was always enough for all – though I have known McAllister, handing round the cream and sugar, hiss in my ear, "Leave some cream for the veesitors"!

Our grandfather died at Loch Goil in the autumn of 1901, and I accompanied Gran to Folkestone, where we stayed in Mr Wampach's comfortable hotel for three months. Gran missed her beloved Alexander sadly, but was very brave. Theirs had been such a perfect marriage, and with their three daughters marrying so young and going to England to live they had been everything to one another for so long. ... For the rest of her widowhood she settled down in Fairlie in a house close to my father's and only went to Loch Goil for a few months in the summer.

Alexander Fergusson's epitaph in the churchyard reads "honourable, good, true".

Neil Campbell and the Armstrong Family

Great efforts have been made by the dogged team of researchers of this history to discover exactly why a water fountain should have been erected in the village in 1882 in memory of Neil Campbell, but no information has come to light. However, Mr Campbell received the following lengthy obituary in the *Dunoon Herald* of 20 September 1879.

A mournful gloom fell over Lochgoilhead on Monday, consequent upon the sudden death of Mr Campbell, merchant and postmaster, in the maturity of his years and public usefulness. His wise and kindly presence has been so familiar for nearly a quarter of a century to the residents and visitors of the loch, that it almost seems as if one of the characteristic and well-known features of the neighbourhood had suddenly disappeared. If to some, at first sight, Mr Campbell might perhaps merely appear a very fair specimen of the douce and canny West Highlandman, the parish of Lochgoilhead and Kilmorich have long recognised and acknowledged the exceptional qualities of his head and heart. Originally intended for the Scotch Kirk, he received an excellent education, and had completed part of the usual university curriculum when his career

4.3 *Lochgoilhead Hotel*

> *was devoted to the pastoral pursuits of his family at Drimsyniebeg Farm. For the last 16 or 18 years, however, he has been best known as merchant and post office master at Lochgoilhead. His early associations naturally attached him to the parish church, in which, during the pastorate of the late Dr Macdougall and of the present popular incumbent, Mr McCorkindale, he was a wise and exemplary elder. Mr Campbell interested himself in everything that concerned the welfare and prosperity of Lochgoilhead. In politics he was an intelligent Conservative, and led the party of Lochgoilhead for Colonel Malcolm at the last parlimentary election. He was also an original member of the 8th Argyllshire Highland Rifles. Mr Campbell, who has been cut off at the comparatively early age of 44 by a severe type of jaundice, has left a widow and four sons, for whom general sympathy is felt and manifested.*

Neil Campbell was born in Lochgoilhead in 1837, the son of James Campbell (1790/91–1850) and Margaret McNaughtan (1805/6–1850). On 29 March 1859 he married Mary Elliot Armstrong, born in Roxburghshire, the daughter of Arthur Armstrong and Margaret Grieve, and the couple had five children: James (*b* 4 Feb 1860), William (*b* 13 Nov 1861), Adam Armstrong (*b* 1 Feb 1865) and twins Duncan and Margaret Elizabeth (*b* 21 Sept 1871). The 1881 census cites Mary Campbell as head postmistress, James as "grocer", William as "telegraph clerk" and Adam and Duncan as "scholar". Margaret Elizabeth had evidently died before her father. There were also two servants, Jessie Ferguson, aged 15, from Blairmore, and Betty Marshall, aged 46, from Tain, Ross & Cromarty. Mary Armstrong died in 1882 at the age of 42.

According to Cathie MacDonald (formerly Armstrong), who used to work in Weir's butcher's shop, Neil Campbell's wife was a member of her family. William Armstrong (1806/7–1888) arrived in the village with his wife Elizabeth and their family in the early 1850s from Newcastleton in the Borders and took over Lochgoilhead Farm (now The Cottage). Apparently six members of the Armstrong family had died of some sort of pestilence that was ravaging the borders at that time. William had two sons, Robert (1850/51–1933) and William (1853/4–1921), and Robert and his wife Christina Barclay, married in 1883, had four sons, William (1885–1960), James Barclay (1888–1957), Robert (1892–1959) and John Nicol (1894–1974). The Armstrongs and the Barclays variously owned Lochgoilhead Hotel (Christina Barclay was listed at the hotel in the 1881 census as a barmaid, when she was living with her parents, James and Catherine Barclay, and Cathie, the daughter of James Barclay Armstrong, was born there); the Armstrongs were also at times at Pole and Corrow farms.

4.4 Robert Armstrong, his wife Christina, and three of their four sons outside The Cottage, early 1900s; the woman standing is probably a domestic servant

John McCallum

On 25 January 1884 John McCallum, the twelve-year-old son of Donald McCallum, a coal merchant in Lochgoilhead, was found guilty of housebreaking and sentenced by Sheriff Cunningham to ten days in Inveraray Jail and three years in a reformatory school. A place was found for him at the Wellington Farm School for boys in Penicuik, and he left Inveraray on board the *Minard Castle* on 11 February.

Kenneth Stewart

The original Rock Cottage in Inverlounin Road was at one time the home of Kenneth Stewart, a master boatbuilder. The slipway near the house, with the slipway rings where the boats were tethered, can still be seen, and the stone foundations remain of the boathouse where Stewart and his workmen plied their trade. Kenneth Stewart was born in Govan, which is probably where he learned his boatbuilding skills (his father, Murdo Stewart, was also a joiner and carpenter), though before settling in Lochgoilhead he and his wife, Jane, lived at Ardkinglas, where their second child was born in 1873. By all accounts his business prospered until October 1878 and the day of the Glasgow bank crash, when he lost all his savings, reputed to be over £600. He evidently did not turn to drink, as he joined the Lochgoilhead Total Abstinence Society after it was set up in February 1882. With a growing family, by 1881 Kenneth and Jane were living at Nuthill, where the census lists them as having seven children; it is probable, however, that Rock Cottage was retained as business premises. Kenneth's declining financial position meant that in late 1882 or early 1883 the family moved away from Lochgoilhead to Govan,

4.5 The original Rock Cottage, painting by Hedwig Knox (later known as Hettie Henderson)

and the master boatbuilder was forced to work as a ship's carpenter. Jane died in October 1883 and the children were farmed out to live with family and friends, though Kenneth married again within five months. Unfortunately he never recovered financially, and he died in the Govan poorhouse in 1901.

Extracts from Notes left by Alexander Campbell

Alexander Campbell was the eldest child of John and Catherine Campbell, who lived at Holly Bank. The 1881 census describes his father as a master shoemaker. It is no wonder that "a good trade was done in shepherds' boots", as the same census lists no fewer than 29 shepherds in the parish. Adam Armstrong, mentioned below, was the third son of Neil and Mary Campbell.

> *I was born in Lochgoilhead on 4th August 1872. My father was boot and shoemaker in the village. Boots at that time were all hand-made – cut and shaped from hide – and took about 2½ days to make. Their cost was in the region of 21/-. A good trade was done in shepherds' boots, and in those days my father always had one or two men working for him. His shop was the place where many people in the village came to spend many happy hours with him, for he was an outstanding man, very quiet and thoughtful in his manner and a good listener; he would never argue with anyone. He was a well-known personality and was respected by all. I never heard him say an angry word. He died at the age of 88. I had also a very fine mother, a hard worker in the home, thrifty and careful, a good and a most attentive wife, and a great help to my father. My father and my mother were God-fearing. Every Sunday morning and evening we had family worship: a psalm was sung, a chapter was read from the Bible and a prayer was said by my father.*
>
> *I have some vivid recollections of school life in the village. The name of the schoolmaster was Mr Smith, and without a doubt he ruled the village. He seemed to think he could do what he liked with the teaching of the children and was at times very severe with his punishment. I remember a parent taking him to court for the punishment he gave his boy but I cannot remember how that case finished. During my schooldays he introduced castor oil as a punishment, and I can assure you that I got my share of it. You got a bottle of castor oil at that time for 1d. At first he had a wine glass,*

4.6 The infamous William "Caster Oil" Smith (1830/31–1914), who inflicted an individual punishment on Lochgoilhead schoolchildren in the 1870s and 1880s

and he would half fill it and force the pupil to take it. I remember a boy by the name of Cameron who is now in a good position in Paisley who would not take it. Mr Smith struck him on the face with the palm of his hand and the boy fell to the floor and broke the glass. Mr Smith did not take another glass into the school, but what he did after that was he caught you by the hair, held back your head and poured the castor oil down your throat. He also got a feather from the wing of a hen, dipped it into the bottle and painted your lips and nose with the oily feather. Now what I am writing here is perfectly true, for I have come through it.

Mr Smith had both tawse and cane which he used most freely. I also remember that he had an invalid wife (his third), and he had a galvanic battery for her use. He took the battery into the school and made the children hold the handle with the wire attached to it, one boy or girl at each end. The others would join hands, and when he worked the battery you felt pins and needles going through you. I remember seeing Cameron getting this for a punishment. Mr Smith made him hold onto the wires with both hands, and when he started working the battery he could only shout and jump. You would have heard the shouts of the boy outside the school, and the schoolmaster just sat on his chair laughing at the state he was in. Many people outside the village wondered what the parents of the scholars were thinking about when they allowed this man to ill-treat their children in this manner. But, as I previously stated, he was a law unto himself and thought he could do what he liked. However, I am glad to say that a Glasgow newspaper got to know about the castor oil punishment and sent a reporter to make inquiries, with the result that a government inspector came and visited the school. Yet nothing was done with him. But the Daily Record went a great length about it and was the means of it being stopped [Castor Oil Smith was in fact dismissed for cruelty after questions were asked in parliament].

I must have left school when I was 11 or 12 years old. During the summer months I spent most of my time at my uncle's farm 3 miles from Lochgoilhead [Beach Farm]. *I was very useful to them there, going for messages to the village, helping with the hay, looking after the cows, and when the sheep had to be gathered in I was up at 2 o'clock in the morning. There were between 700 and 800 sheep on the farm and they had to be clipped and dipped. During lambing time you had to be continually on the hills. I must say I had a good training from my two uncles who looked after the farm, which now belongs to Glasgow Corporation and has been turned into a plantation of trees. There are thousands upon thousands of young trees planted on the hillsides: it will take 40 to 50 years before they will be ready for cutting down.*

I walked every part of those hills from the point as you enter the loch right up to the head of the loch – about 6 miles. At a cairn near the top of the hill called Belachen Dorest there are dangerous holes. I used to get stones and throw them down, and you could hear the stones knocking against the sides for fully a minute, giving you an idea of the depth of the hole. About the hillside and rocks during my time there were wild goats: they were sure-footed, and it was wonderful how they could jump from rock to rock without any trouble. There would be about twenty of them, and they always kept together. When you wanted the skin or head of a buck goat they had to be shot – they could not be captured, they were so wild.

I spent many happy days with my uncles and aunts on this farm. They were most generous to all who came to see them, and they were well known for their hospitality all over the countryside. While on the farm I also learned how to handle rowing boats, for there were two always at your disposal. I thought nothing about rowing the boat 3 miles to Lochgoilhead and back again, and I have seen me out with it when the wind was so strong that I could not make any headway.

When I was 13 years old I became a message boy to merchants by the name of Jackson, near the pier. I was Jack-of-all-trades in this shop, helping in the bakehouse and going round the district with pony and van. I had to go down to the cellar, bottle the beer, cork it and label it. Not a very nice job for a boy of my age. My wage was 3/6d per week, with dinner and tea.

When I was 14 I was engaged with Armstrong, who had Lochgoilhead Farm. I had all kinds of work to do, going with the milk morning and evening and looking after a dozen good milk

4.7 Weavers' cottages at the head of the loch

part of the hills, so I was a poacher that day.

I remember another incident which took place on a Sunday with my friend Adam. The old church minister went to Cairndow to preach occasionally and the Free Church minister went over once a month. On this particular Sunday, Adam was driving the old church minister and I was driving the Free Church one. What brotherly love those ministers showed to each other! This Sunday I was driving Mr Gibson over to Cairndow in the afternoon and Adam was driving Mr McCorkindale back to Lochgoilhead, for he had been preaching in the forenoon. Driving through Hell's Glen there are no houses for miles, and when I got to the top of the hill which looks into Loch Fyne, who did I see coming up the other side but Adam and Mr McCorkindale. The roads were very bad and narrow, so when I came to a good part of the road I stopped to allow Adam to pass safely. But this is what Mr Gibson said to me: "Drive on, Alex, drive on, and don't look at that man"– meaning the other minister. What I should have done was to drive on and put him in the ditch, for he deserved it. Yet coming back that night he preached to me all the way, telling me about many young people dying. Yes, that was the feeling that existed between the old church and the Free. He, the minister, went into the hotel and got his tea, but he did not think that I could do with a cup of tea also. His servant gave me a bit of cake before I left, but no tea for the driver!

When I was 16 I was asked by Mr Crawford of Pole Farm to go to a place 3 miles from Bathgate to assist his shepherd to look after 400 hogs – sheep nine months old. This was my first experience away from home. Everything was new to me, and I was even interested in seeing a train going along the line. In October that year, when I had just turned 17, I was asked to go to Langbank for a period of six months with 280 sheep. I went, and my father and mother were quite anxious about me going out there myself. I remember my clothes were packed in a very smart box of my father's. I went by the steamer "Edinburgh Castle" to Princes Pier. The sheep were taken off there and we had to travel on foot with them to Langbank. A shepherd came out with me and helped to get them through the streets of Greenock and Port Glasgow. I had a good collie dog to assist me. I would have been helpless without her.

The name of the farmer which I was to stay with for six months was a Mr Hamilton. He was getting on in years and didn't do very much farm work himself, but he could take a good dram. He had two farms and the name of the farm the sheep wintered on was Garscale. You can see the hill exactly opposite Dumbarton. The sheep went up to the hilltop at night and during the day I would take them down to the arable parks, where they got a good feeding. I gained great experience during my spell at Langbank and returned to Lochgoilhead to work for a short time with Mr Crawford at Pole Farm.

In 1890 I left Lochgoilhead to settle in Clydebank. I was employed with Singer Manuf. Co from 1890 until I retired in 1942.

Lochgoil's Emigrants to the Colonies

The economic depression following the Napoleonic Wars in the early part of the nineteenth century caused considerable unemployment, particularly among Scottish weavers, whose weekly income fell from 25s. in 1803 to 5s. 5d. by 1819. Farm labourers were also affected, as the price of grain fell sharply. Conditions were particularly bad in Lanarkshire and Renfrewshire, and a number of societies were formed there to encourage emigration to the colonies. Several thousand people travelled from Greenock to Canada to what became known as Lanark County, in present-day Ontario, where each man who had reached the age of 19 was given 100 acres of land, and families received building materials, tools, bedding, rations, seeds and financial loans for the first year. Prospective immigrants had to pay for their own passage, though most were in fact assisted by funds raised through public subscription. Because more applied for assistance than funds could support, places were decided by lottery.

The first such emigrants in search of a better life crossed the Atlantic in three ships in 1820. Among the 607 passengers who left Greenock on board the *Earl of Buckinghamshire* on 29 April 1821 were Duncan McDougall, a farmer from Lochgoilhead, with his wife, Ann, and their five children. Duncan and his cousin Archibald had applied for passage via the Parkhurst Emigration Society. The voyage took 48 days, and the passengers had to endure being grounded off Ireland as well as storms en route before they arrived in Quebec on 16 June. They were then taken to Montreal by steamship, from thence to Lachine, and from Lachine to Prescott on the St Lawrence River by flat-bottomed boat. The final part of the journey, which took five days, was made by wagon over rough trails. The McDougalls settled in North Sherbrooke township, and having previously worked on the land evidently adapted better to the hardships of the pioneer life than those who had been weavers or tradesmen.

Later emigrants from Lochgoilhead to North Sherbrooke, and possibly members of the same family, were Alexander McDougall, born at Ardnahein and baptised at Lochgoilhead Church on 12 November 1778, and his wife, Janet Clark. They had married in 1803 and had ten children. Together with Janet's mother, the 80-year-old Margaret McKellar Clark, they left Greenock on board the *Nailer* in 1828. Alexander was described as "shepherd in Coromonachan" in the parish register on the baptism of the couple's children, and he also seems to have adapted well to the farming life; the eighth generation of his descendants continue to work the same land and to live in the house built by Alexander and Janet's son Alexander.

Chapter Five
Into the Twentieth Century

It seems that the importance of Lochgoilhead in the eighteenth century was a result of the fact that it lay on the main route from northern and central Argyll to Glasgow, Edinburgh and the south. Before modern methods of transportation, people journeyed on horseback or on foot and crossed rivers and lochs in small boats. What was known as the Duke's Path passed through Lochgoilhead and then crossed the hill to Mark, where there was a ferry, and people travelling onwards from Inveraray would probably have used the village as one of their principal resting places. With the arrival of steam Lochgoilhead became even more important, as it enjoyed a better steamer service than many places, and until the opening of the Callander and Oban Railway, and later the West Highland Railway, Lochgoilhead remained on the main route from Oban to Glasgow.

5.1 The Rest and Be Thankful, c1920s

In 1833 Wordsworth visited the area, having come from Oban, by Loch Awe, to Inveraray. He alluded to the Rest and be Thankful stone:

Doubling and doubling with laborious walk,
Who that has gained at length the wished for height,
This brief, this simple wayside call can slight,
And rest not thankful!

Later he journeyed through Hell's Glen and on to Greenock:

We have not passed into a doleful city,
We who were led to-day down a grim dell,
By some too boldly called "the jaws of Hell".

In the early part of the nineteenth century Glasgow, which was benefiting from the Industrial Revolution, began to expand at an enormous rate. One problem encountered was that of the supply and demand of food, and the herring fishermen throughout Argyll were affected. The boats which operated on Loch Fyne were faced with a long and dangerous trip through the Kyles of Bute into the River Clyde, a distance of about 90 miles. As demand for herring grew, it was decided that a more direct route of transportation was needed, and so the "Herring Roads" were built. One of the first of these was the road into Lochgoilhead through Hell's Glen (others were constructed through Glendaruel to Colintraive and by Loch Eck to Ardentinny). Road building at that time was not exactly simple: even the famous engineer Thomas Telford found that highland rains and melting snow could bring down floods far beyond his early calculations, and it appears that the bridge on the Lochgoil road was so badly constructed at first that it fell five times. However, once the road was completed, the fish from Loch Fyne could be offloaded, transported by road to Loch Goil and then transferred to one of the numerous boats plying for trade to make the relatively short trip of some 30 miles to Glasgow.

George Houston

Argyll was an important painting ground for George Houston, one of Scotland's most important landscape artists, in the early years of the twentieth century. The Houston family spent the summers at Lochgoilhead, where they rented first the school house in the village and then, from 1904, Drimsyniebeg Farm. In those days they travelled by train from Glasgow to Greenock and took the paddle steamer from there to Lochgoilhead, where a horse and trap would have conveyed them to the farm. It was there that Houston's third son, Edward, was born in August 1904. Lochgoilhead was chosen partly because of the commercial opportunities it offered. In the nineteenth century many prosperous Glasgow families had built villas in the area so that they could escape from the bustle of the city. The road through Glen Goil and Hell's Glen to Loch Fyne was an important commercial and tourist route, and the locality was thus familiar to Houston's Glasgow purchasers. Between 1904 and 1910 he exhibited eleven watercolours and one oil painting at the Royal Scottish Society of Painters in Watercolours, at least five of which were of Lochgoilhead and Glen Goil. In 1936 Glasgow Corporation bought Houston's *Heart of Argyll* for its permanent collection. This is a view of the road from St Catherine's on Loch Fyne towards Hell's Glen.

The widow of Houston's son John, a pilot, and their young daughter chose to retire to Crag, on Inverlounin Road, after her husband's accidental death at the age of 45. Her parents, Mr and Mrs Stephenson, owned the house and had previously used it as a holiday home.

***

EXTRACTS FROM A LETTER WITH VILLAGE NEWS FROM LOCHGOILHEAD,
March 1904

My dear mother,

It is now twenty to eleven and we are just now in from the soiree — scandalous isn't it, but really it was good. Greenock things are not in it ... The hall was packed, there being 130 present — the biggest audience they ever had.

When the Edinburgh arrived today it was minus the pastries for the soiree, and you can guess the consternation. As Mr Campbell [the minister] *said, "They had to put all their heads together", after which they went to Mr and Mrs Jackson and MacDonalds and told them to "scrape all they could of biscuits etc to make up the bags". We got a bag each on going in but had to give them up to the children so got nothing. They only provided for 110 and 130 turned up.*

We could write loads but will keep till we turn up because it's so late, but I though a little was better than nothing.

I remain your loving daughter ...

***

Drimsynie Estate

The present house at Drimsynie was built by the Neilson family around the mid-1850s to replace the original house, which was much smaller and situated further south than the existing building. James Beaumont Neilson, an engineer, was made manager of the Glasgow Gas Works at a young age and had patented the hot blast process in 1828. The house had its own carbide gas works and a sawmill with a waterwheel. There were also iron fences and bridges which had been brought in from Glasgow by puffer. Alongside the estate buildings forming the courtyard was a very large walled garden, measuring approximately 300 by 200 yards. Until around the mid-1900s the estate was managed traditionally, and employed gamekeepers, rabbit-catchers and gardeners. The owners took great pride in the well-laid-out formal gardens, and they imported and planted varied and rare species of trees, including beech, both cut leaf and curly leaf, rarely seen today, copper beech and walnut. Duncan Henderson recalls his grandfather, William Henderson, relating to him how one day in the late 1800s he met the boat to collect some rare saplings, so small they fitted in his game bag, which was slung over his shoulder. They were planted at the bottom of Drimsynie Avenue. These magnificent sequoias are sadly the only remaining specimens from a once beautiful estate.

5.2 Drimsynie House, mid-1850s, with members of the Neilson family

On the grassy area south of the current car park at Drimsynie is situated a large rock, popular as a climbing spot with visiting children. This rock was once known as Cannon Rock because in the 1800s it housed a large cannon, which faced south towards the loch. Two pieces of protruding metal remain embedded in the rock.

Drimsynie was a popular venue for fishermen and shooting parties. Estate records for the season 1904 show the total catch of fish from the Drimsynie side of the river over a four-month period as:

salmon	*40*
sea trout	*126*
yellow trout	*321*

and in the same year the following game was bagged:

grouse	*2*
blackgame	*1*
pheasant	*273*
woodcock	*19*
snipe	*3*
wild fowl	*1*
hares	*2*
rabbits	*2145*
roe deer	*1*

Although roe deer were fairly common, red deer did not frequent the hills around Loch Goil until the planting of conifers started in the early 1900s. As the trees matured and offered cover and protection, so the red deer began to appear. The first sighting of a stag was recorded in 1908. In *The Book of the Red Deer,* edited by John Ross, Alexander Patience wrote that he shot an eight-

5.3 Keepers at Drimsynie showing off their pheasant bag, early 1900s; William Henderson is on the far right

pointer stag, one of a band of four, on the Ardgoil hill tops in October 1921. Included is a photograph of the antlers, which were unusual in not having forked tips.

5.4 A shooting party at Drimsynie, early 1900s

The Neilsons continued to use Drimsynie as a holiday home until about 1920, when a Mr Black bought it and the Neilsons took over Corriesyke. Major Methven then owned the house, and a seat in the village car park has a memorial plaque to Mrs Isabella Grove, wife of Brigadier I. R. Grove, who is referred to as "chatelaine of Drimsynie during World War II". After the war the house was bought by an industrialist, Mr Pyman, and it was purchased about 1955 by the Forestry Commission. It was later run as a hotel by the Alexander family, who sold it in 1980 to Douglas Campbell.

Fox and Rabbit Trapping in the Glens

In the *Statistical Accounts* of the 1790s and of 1845 references were made to the high population in the area of foxes, and their levels were controlled by the regular visits of itinerant fox hunters (Davy MacLachlan's father was a fox hunter). Possibly because of this rigorous control, by the late 1800s the rabbit population in the glens around Loch Goil exploded. Rabbit hunting and trapping was carried out on a very regular basis until the 1950s, when the onset of myxomatosis all but eradicated the problem. (Unfortunately it also had devastating effects on the indigenous wildlife, whose food source they were; most noticeably the wild-cat and eagle populations were decimated.) Before this disease took its toll, as one report states, any sudden noise would disturb so many rabbits that the ground would appear to be alive with them.

Drimsynie was one of the properties in the area that farmed a large number of sheep and so gave work to itinerant fox hunters, and at least six rabbit catchers were employed by the estate. They would lay their snares at night and collect their catch every day. A pair of rabbits weighed an average of 5 lbs, and it was not unusual for these men to carry down from the hills on their shoulders a hundredweight of rabbits. Of course in those days the hills were not covered in conifers as they are today. The rabbits were hung in large wicker hampers before being shipped to butchers in Glasgow.

5.5 *Jock MacPherson, shepherd at Monevechadan, with his dogs by Moses' Well, 1925*

Locals from the Loch Goil area and across the hills to Strachur would also gather and work together as a team to hunt rabbits, foxes and other vermin, with some driving the animals through the glens and passes to the snares and guns of the others. Some of the participants would have regular places where they would lie in wait, and these locations became known by such names as the Minister's Rock or Duncy Pat's Stone. (Duncy Pat was a McKellar from Strachur who used to drive the animals from the Strachur side and into Glen Canachadan.) High on the flank of Mullach Coire a' Chuir in Glen Canachadan, not too far above the recently built forest road, is a "cave" or shelter in which the hunters stored their snares on wooden stakes wedged into the rocks. These stakes are still in place, along with the initials of some of the hunters scratched into the rocks.

Hangman's Knoll

The story goes that there was once a gibbet on the Hell's Glen road, at the point overlooking Loch Fyne towards Inveraray. Condemned prisoners from Inveraray Jail were brought across the loch to meet their end at Hangman's Knoll, and their last sight on earth was therefore the view of Inveraray. It was believed that in death they could never return to that place, as spirits were unable to travel across water. Even today many travellers in Hell's Glen experience an unexplained chill as they pass the spot where the gibbet stood.

***

MORE VILLAGE NEWS, 1926

Written by Hayward Maclean, the 15-year-old son of the minister

The Manse of Lochgoilhead
10th March 1926

Dear Tom

I am alone with my solitary self, deserted by all, Mother and Dad being away from home, and I have not even a cat to comfort me in my desolation; therefore I decide to write a letter to somebody. The place is beginning to awake from its winter dormancy and quiescence – a man arrived in a motor car today. There is a very strong chance of a morning and evening steamer being put on for the summer.

A landslide took place on the "rest" owing to the heavy floods, and it nearly carried away John Bell the road-man's house. It will take easily a week to clear the road, as it is one of the worst that we have ever experienced.

Dad and I were over in Edinburgh the other day, and on returning we stuck on the "rest" owing to the depth of snow, and we also had no chains, which made the ascent impossible. We motored the whole way.

...

Yours
H. Gillian Maclean

P.S. It is genuine about the steamer.

***

Quarry Brae

As one drives out of the village towards Carrick Castle, just after crossing the bridge the road inclines to an awkward humped blindspot. This little hump is called Quarry Brae because the area immediately to the right, which is now covered in trees, was a working quarry until around the 1920s. Before the days of excavating equipment the labourers worked in threes – two men either side of the working rock face wielding huge hammers and the third turning the chisel.

Pole Farm

In the nineteenth century Pole flats was mostly agricultural land and was used mainly for growing hay. However, each year, because of heavy rain, the river would burst its banks just around haymaking time. The newly built haystacks would be washed down the river and eventually ended up on the loch. It was therefore reckoned that drastic action was needed, and the decision was taken to straighten the river and reinforce its banks. The onerous task was completed in 1884, on the same day that Dougie Cameron's father was born. Unfortunately, over the years the banks of the river eroded, and by the 1950s it was not unusual to catch sight once more of a haystack floating on the loch. Sometimes one would become wedged under the bridge, causing the river to flood.

5.6 Haymaking at Pole Farm, early 1920s

Before the days of modern sheep dips, sheep were treated against pests and insects in a smearing shed. Their fleeces were parted along the back and sides and a buttery substance called *smiorach* was applied, the theory being that the gooey mixture would melt and run with the heat from the animals' bodies, offering total protection. Carved on the wall of an outhouse at Pole Farm, under a plaque of a tup's head, are the Gaelic words "Tigh na smiorach" – "smearing shed".

Ian Morrison

The Christian missionary Ian Morrison, who died in 2004, spent his childhood at Beach Farm, near Stuckbeg. He was born at Ardeonaig, on the south side of Loch Tay, where his father was a shepherd. Having moved first to Ardnamurchan and then to Glen Croe, in 1920 the family, which was Gaelic speaking, settled at Beach Farm. Ian and his brothers attended Lochgoilhead school, walking the three miles each way every day. Hugh Cameron-White's mother often stayed during the school holidays with the MacNicols at Stuckbeg, and she and her brothers used to spend a lot of time playing with the Morrison boys. She remembers vividly that there was an old grandfather with a big white beard who used to say grace before meals. She also said that the Morrison boys were awful swearers ("the very worst words"), and there was a lot of talk when Ian Morrison went in for the ministry. Ian left school at the age of 14 to work for an engineering firm in Glasgow. When he was about 20 he became a member of the evangelical Glasgow Tabernacle and began preaching on street corners, and shortly afterwards he attended the Bible Training Institute to gain a diploma in theology. In 1936 he went to China as a missionary. There he married his wife Rachel, herself the daughter of missionaries in China, and learned to read and write Mandarin. Although his family left for Canada before the attack on Pearl Harbor, Ian spent four years in a Japanese internment camp. From 1948 to 1965 he was in Singapore as general secretary of the Bible societies in Malaya, responsible for the translation and distribution of scripture into the many languages of Singapore, Malaya and Borneo. Thereafter, until his retirement in 1977, he worked in Scotland. According to his obituarist in the *Glasgow Herald*, the Revd David Torrance, Ian Morrison "had inherited the traits of determined single-mindedness, integrity, hard work and unswerving duty that were characteristic of many a west-Highland chield of his generation, and these were evidenced in much of his life."

Lochgoilhead: Shopping Mecca

Supplies of food came from various people in the village at various different times. The general store owned by David Smith was burnt to the ground in 1929, an event that was reported in a local newspaper:

LOCHGOILHEAD BLAZE

An alarming fire occurred last night in Lochgoilhead when the shop belonging to Mr David Smith, general merchant, with bakery at the back, was completely destroyed. The fire was discovered about eight o'clock and burned for fully two hours. Villagers made a gallant attempt to quell the outbreak. There was a strong wind and it was only with difficulty that adjoining buildings were saved. The shop was completely gutted.

The site was later occupied by Fulton's Stores, which was demolished in 1992.

5.7 Fulton's Stores, just before the building was demolished

Jackson's was the main store at the pierhead in the early part of the century; this later became Robertson's and by the 1950s was Wylie's. Duncan Henderson was born and brought up over the pierhead stores, at which time the shop was run by Jimmy Cunningham. In the 1930s and 1940s groceries could also be bought at McLeod's general store, next to the post office. Donald McLeod, who had a thick, flowing red beard and a large, jolly smiling face, owned a delivery van which, apart from arriving late at night, had a back door that was seldom shut, so he spent a good deal of time recovering various items from the road. According to Cathie MacDonald he used to invite people in for tea. He had a room and bed at the back of the shop, as he used to stay in Lochgoilhead during the week and go home to Alexandria at

5.8 The interior of Ronnie McLeod's shop, late 1950s

the weekends. Cathie also reckoned that before McLeod took over the shop it was Moscadini's ice cream store.

During the days of food rationing Ronnie McLeod, who took over the shop from his father in about 1949 or 1950, kept little treats under the counter for his favourite customers, but the best treats, such as ham bones, were kept hidden under the bed in the back room. Nera Wigham recalled that, in the 1960s, his shop sold the best cheese and bacon you could get anywhere.

Early in the twentieth century the butcher was Donald Fraser. When he was in his teens Dougie Cameron worked with Fraser's successor, Jock Weir, at which point the shop (up beyond the pier at Planetree) was a butcher's and general stores. There was a slaughterhouse behind, and all the animals that were intended for slaughter were kept in "Butcher's Park" – the field immediately north of the second bridge. Weir had competition, however, as Johnny Bell's van came to the village once or twice a week. Weir lived in Creaganiver, but previously he had travelled in daily from Ardno, bringing milk to the steading at The Cottage. One day, when he was turning in front of his shop, his van went right over the edge of the road and into the loch. (The same thing later happened to the builders of Mingulay.)

5.9 *The smiddy, c1920s*

5.10 *Jack Munro the blacksmith outside the smiddy; the boy may be his son Andrew*

5.11 Alec Boyd with his mother and Mr and Mrs McKellar outside the tearoom and sweetie shop, mid-1930s

Cathie MacDonald worked in Weir's shop before it was taken over by Gillespie. When Gillespie went to open a shop in Inveraray, George Law took over the business and moved it from Planetree to the old school house in the centre of the village.

Both Creaganiver and the pierhead stores had bakeries attached to them at some point. Lotty McEwan ran a haberdashery across the road from the pier. There was a tearoom beside Fulton's Stores and another run by Jackie Boyd's grandmother, which was next to Jackie Boyd's cottage in Hall Road. There was also a sweetie shop there run by Mr and Mrs McKellar. In the 1940s Nellie Hall had a sweetie shop at Cruachan.

Jack Munro the blacksmith operated from the smiddy next door to the church. The smiddy was the most popular meeting place for a chat and a bit of gossip, especially in the winter, as the forge was always going. There was a small dairy situated just before you came round the corner to the hotel (the steading attached to The Cottage).

Heckie Blair was the fishmonger. He kept nets in the loch and came round selling fish from a basket. However, it seems that fish were then plentiful in the loch, and you had only to drop a line into the water while taking a trip on the steamer to get a least a bucketful. Heckie and his brother Duncan hired out pleasure boats in competition with each other from opposite sides of

Lochgoilhead Pier but never spoke to each other. In addition to his farming interests, John "Bash" Blair was the local undertaker for many years. He and his assistants would wash down the body, dress it and place it in the coffin, and arrange the internment.

5.12 George Eadie with Mrs Middleton (Duncan Henderson's grandmother), one of his weavers, 1947

Weaving also took place in the village. George Eadie, formerly a Clyde shipowner, who lived at Creaganiver, helped to put Lochgoilhead on the industrial map in the 1940s through his production of tweed on handlooms. According to a newpaper article in *The Bulletin* of 12 April 1947, the material was of a texture and variety that had attracted the notice of leading fashion houses all over the country. In any event, the workers were earning more than they would have in Glasgow. At that point Mr Eadie was expanding his business – looms were situated at least at Creaganiver and in the top half of what had previously been Jackson's stores – but evidently the enterprise did not last much longer, as the owner died in 1950.

There was a post office at Douglas Pier in addition to the one in the village (at one point the village post office was situated at Creaganiver). The *Comet,* which came up from Gourock every day, arrived first at Douglas Pier and then went on to Lochgoilhead, fetching and carrying mail and other provisions, as well as passengers. John Neilson remembers when the postmaster-general first proposed to take the *Comet* off the route and transport the mail by bus. A friend of his father's, Fred Turner, composed a poem about the situation:

As citizens of Lochgoilhead in the county of Argyll
Are you not very worried that in a little while
It would appear the PMG intends (so says the press)
To discontinue sailing of that maritime express
The Comet, which for years and years has sailed to Lochgoilhead.
No longer will she carry mails; they'll go by road instead.
I can picture Christmas numbers of 1938
Depicting in a lurid way why Lochgoil mails are late
No, not from any storm at sea or from a strike ashore
But simply owing to the fact the Rest is covered yet
With frost-bound snows and drifts piled high
While up above the Cobbler winks his eye
Ha-ha, he-he, it really makes him laugh
To watch the fruitless efforts of a staff
Of sweeping roadmen working all they know
To find and dig a mailvan from the snow.

Fortunately there was a compromise, and the *Comet* remained in service for a few years longer.

5.13 The Comet, which served Lochgoilhead until 1946

The Bouquet Garni

The pierhead stores were bought in November 1973 by Mike and Brenda Dimmer and their 14-day-old son Quentin. After the birth of their second son, Austin, in 1976, the old-style village shop was converted into a mini supermarket and the "back shop" into a veritable cornucopia of bargain goods. However, the family had spotted the need for a small restaurant, and the Bouquet Garni was born in June 1977. It rapidly gained fame and secured "Taste of Scotland" approval. Mike and Brenda entered a competition to prove that they ran the best small independent business in Britain. They won the regional heat, and the whole of Scotland heat, and were flown to London to pick up the national runners-up prize. A year later they won a family holiday in the Cayman Islands, having proved that their restaurant in "remote" Lochgoilhead was the best in Britain at marketing turtle meat.

Many of the tables were booked every Saturday by regulars, yachtsmen sailed in from afar, and lots of local hoteliers were frequent guests. On several occasions, when the submarine returned from its tours of duty, the restaurant was fully booked by the officers of HMS *Renown* for their "ladies' night out", and it provided for the needs of the officers and gentlemen crew of HMS *Invincible* when the carrier was on trials in the loch. The atmosphere was totally unique. The musical entertainment was wide and varied, starring Hillees Elastic Band from Tarbert. Locals Terry Bateman and the Cushbarry Band were hugely popular, and Martin Karter was a frequent visitor. Trevor was resident pianist for some time. Impromptu skiffle sessions also became a source of great entertainment. Among the highlights over the years were the visits by a talented team of Greek dancers from Glasgow. Often dinners were served early to allow the famous "slides to music" presentation by Derek Prescott, and "intercourse quiz nights" were popular until customers discovered that it consisted of questions between courses. There were also many theme nights, involving fancy dress. You could even hire a scooter from the restaurant to tour the area.

Among the dishes featured at the Bouquet Garni were steaks served on sizzling bull platters, lots of locally caught fish from Kenny Wilson, rabbit bred especially for the restaurant by a farm in Strachur (Bright Eyes Casserole), the aforementioned turtle meat (Turtle Stroganoff, Turtle Burgers, Real (not mock) Turtle Soup, etc), Goilash Vera Lynn ("veal meat again"), and thick chicken broth (they were never the brightest of birds). The menu, presented as a scroll, became highly prized for its puns and reflected the fun aspect of eating. Remember the lobster in the cherry tree?

It was in 1989 that a major expansion took place, the result of a big investment by Leslie Cuthbertson, with the restaurant moving upstairs where the Dimmers' house was and the old restaurant becoming Herb's Wine Bar, remembered for a vast range of beers, crisps, wines and spirits and interesting things happening. Many staff members are also fondly remembered, among them Sue Prescott, Elaine Turnbull, Isobel Leeper, Susie Cuthbertson, Yvonne, Linda and Alison McAulay, Gary McCorkill, Margaret Cox, Juanella Marchant, Yvette Hayes, Margaret Tweedlie, Karen Gillespie, Fiona Phillips, Mark Evans, Julie Campbell, Jackie McKinlay, Ingrid and Nathan Gurevitch, Jean Ferguson, Ann and Tony Birdsall, Wendy and Angus Neill, Elspeth Ratcliffe, Fiona Dempster, May Kelbie, Damien McCartan, Debbie Sim, Brenda Adams and Deborah Fyfe, plus several other part-timers and catering college students. The association lasted until 1992, when Mike started his Mike the Knife mobile sharpening service and left the restaurant to Leslie, who later leased it for a few years to Bill Brett.

The end of an era was sealed in 2001, when the building was sold with permission to convert it into a three-bedroom house.

The Original Swimming Pool

Before the village knew the luxury of a real swimming pool, local children were taught to swim at the pier by Jock Paige. It started when Jock was asked

5.14 The original swimming pool

to teach the two bored children of a regular holidaymaker. From there it snowballed until most of the children in the village were taking lessons. Eventually annual swimming galas were held, and the children earned certificates, medals and cups for their efforts. The library now holds the silver cup, sponsored by Mrs Henrietta Forman of The Lodge, that is engraved with the winners' names between the years 1954 and 1963. Among the successful children are two well-known locals: Catriona MacCallum (MacInnes) and Gordon Alexander, who won it in 1958 and 1962 respectively. Apparently Jock's swimming attire was a feature in itself: it was the knitted woollen type, but it had been darned so many times over the years that it resembled a patchwork quilt.

Law and Order

In November 1950 Constable Neil John McCallum arrived in Lochgoilhead. He obviously did not make himself too popular, for he was a stickler for the letter of the law when it came to such matters as parked cars being required to have their side lights on. When he found Sleith the builder parked in his van with no lights he gave him a warning, little knowing that Dr MacIntyre, the local GP, was in the back with a large stag they had acquired!

On another occasion two villagers returning from a wedding in Cairndow, where they had had rather too many drams, crashed their car near Pole Farm. No one was hurt, but Constable McCallum arrived on the scene and put the two men in the police van. He woke Dr MacIntyre at 4 a.m. to have the driver tested for being under the influence of alcohol. In those pre-breathalyser days the usual test was to ask the suspect to walk in a straight line. Dr MacIntyre got him to walk along the edge of his carpet and pronounced him sober. Constable McCallum, not satisfied with this decision, took them up Inverlounin Road to the home of Dr Stalker and woke her for a second opinion. Much to his chagrin Dr Stalker set the same test and also pronounced the driver sober.

In August 1952 Constable McCallum was transferred to Oban following a trial at Dunoon sheriff court (the proceedings of which are recorded in the *Dunoon Observer* of 26 July), where he was found guilty of "falsely and maliciously accusing a Lochgoilhead farmer of a criminal offence". It was alleged that he had fabricated evidence against Bash Blair for allowing his cows to wander on the road. While it seems that there had been complaints at various times concerning Blair's cattle, on this occasion Constable McCallum, evidently frustrated at being unable to nail his man, had driven the seven offending cows along the road to the spot where his "witnesses" were. Sheriff Donald said that "perverting the ends of justice was a thing which no court would tolerate for a moment. The general circumstances were almost ridiculous, like the subject of a short story about Para Handy." He imposed a fine of £15 with the alternative of sixty days.

5.15 Archibald MacDonald, the policeman in Lochgoilhead from 1945 to 1950

The police constable before Constable McCallum was Archibald MacDonald, a Gaelic speaker from Skye, who was stationed in Lochgoilhead from 1945 to 1950. He covered Lochgoilhead, Carrick Castle, and Mark on Loch Long, and he also relieved the Arrochar policeman. Once a year he visited Mark to see Jock MacDonald, the sole tenant, to check his farm animals, and he went armed with a gift of freshly baked scones made by his mother. A report of this visit appeared in the *Sunday Post* written by Frances Gay, who accompanied the constable. They chartered a motor boat driven by David MacLachlan from Douglas Pier.

According to MacDonald's daughter, Christina:

> *The police station was situated in Viewfield Terrace with a large metal plate coloured navy blue and white stating "Police Station". My father's office was situated in a corner of our sitting-room with telephone in the hall. I can remember a very serious car accident while he was relieving the Arrochar policeman. It involved a honeymoon couple who mistook the River Croe for the road (while under flood) at the foot of the Rest and Be Thankful. Bodies from the wrecked Standard Vanguard car were recovered several days later when the flood subsided. I have photos taken by National Press to substantiate this.*
>
> *At one end of Viewfield Terrace lived the Cameron family – they were forestry workers – and at the pier end the house belonged to a Glasgow furrier who came on holiday there. Our next-door neighbour was an 80-odds year old Mrs Anderson who belonged to*

Skye also. She had been married several times and did all her own roof repairs in her long black clothing. The man that did repairs to our house was a Hughie Sleith and also a Mr MacCallum, who was a builder.

I can remember my father having a very serious accident on his bike while on duty returning from Carrick Castle. A stag was startled as my father passed and the animal darted into the path of the bicycle, throwing my father up in the air, and he landed heavy on the road. He lay there unconscious, bleeding badly and severely injured, until the Admiralty lorry came along. He was stretchered onto the lorry, taken home and the doctor called. I can remember him swathed in bandages due to head and face injuries; a bone stuck out from his elbow, so he wore a sling, and his leg was cut. His uniform was torn and bloodsoaked. He was off work due to his injuries and my mum and I were most upset.

I can remember my father curling somewhere in Lochgoilhead, and he was part of a team which travelled now and then to Crossmyloof.

Douglas Campbell and Drimsynie

Douglas Campbell was born in Greenock, the youngest of three sons. His father owned butchers' shops in Greenock and also farms in Strachur, where the family lived. Douglas attended Strachur primary school and a private secondary school, but his father died when he was fifteen, forcing him to return in 1950 to assist his brothers in running the leased farm of Strachur Mhor. The farm was very basic: his steading was initially an old railway carriage and he had to build his own sheep fank and steading. Neighbouring farmers were impressed and contracted him to build sheep fanks for them. This led to other building work, including the steading at Carrick Farm for Peter Ferguson, and the Forestry Commission also gave him building contracts. Little did he know that this would lead to his eventually forming the building firm Lochgoilhead Developments, nowadays known as Drimsynie Construction. His next venture was to lease Corrow Farm in May 1962. This encompassed fields on the north side of Loch Goil, west of the Glaslett burn where the caravan site is now. Following tradition when a farm changed hands, the sheep were rounded up, counted and marked – a large undertaking for one day and in which local volunteers joined. This was a big social occasion, with lunch for the helpers provided in the farmhouse followed by a ceilidh in the evening.

Captain George Pound, who lived at Inverlounin, was the son of the famous first sea lord Dudley Pound (1877–1943), who commanded with distinction the battleship *Colossus* at the battle of Jutland in 1916 and for the remaining two years of the First World War directed operations at the Admiralty. George Pound was a champion of the sea scout movement and for some years, beginning in 1967, held sea scout camps in his garden (see Chapter 9, Lochgoilhead Centre). At this time the shelter park, which was part of Ardgoil Estate and previously owned by Glasgow Corporation, was the property of the Forestry Commission and was used for holiday caravans. In order that the sea scouts could continue to hold camps in the village, Sir Michael Noble of Ardkinglas, then secretary of state for Scotland, and the director of the Forestry Commission approached Douglas Campbell to allow the transfer of the caravans to the Corrow Farm fields along the north side of the loch. Douglas agreed on condition that he should run the caravan site, which hence emerged in its present form; it has since expanded over a larger area and now includes chalets and lodges. The first warden of the site was Tommy Rhind, who had previously been the roadman.

Douglas Campbell's next acquisition was the Carrick Hotel, a joint venture in 1972 with Peter Ferguson. Drimsynie House was purchased in 1980 from the Alexander family. At that time it was a simple eight-bedroom hotel, but nowadays it boasts many facilities, among them a 25 metre swimming pool, a curling rink and indoor bowling. The Lochgoilhead Hotel was purchased from Rangers Football Club in 1984. Whereas Douglas hired his first employee, a shepherd, in 1963, today his company employs in the region of 200 people.

Douglas and Jean Campbell were married in 1959 and have three sons who, with their respective wives, are very much involved in various aspects of the company. While Jean has always played a major role, she manages to find time to be very much involved in village life. She is a member of the church board and a long-serving committee member of the SWRI, and she organizes almost single-handedly all the events and teams for the Drimsynie Ladies Curling Club.

The Lochgoilhead Hill Race

The hill race up the Steeple (1257 ft) was started by the Revd Harry Thomson in 1960, when the winner, a Mr D. Watt, made the ascent and descent in 26 minutes. That year a number of children took part in the juniors' race – Gordon Alexander, Andy Hammon, Margaret Laurie, Hammy McGuire, Alistair McNicol, Alistair Mather, Willie Mather, Marion Montgomery,

Eric Smart, Tony Smithman, and Sheila Urquhart; Hammy McGuire was the boys' winner, and Margaret Laurie took the laurels for the girls. The following year saw a slower time – 29 minutes 15 seconds, by Mr D. Wood – but the records kept from 1978 show faster times. John Fisher, who won the race on four occasions, achieved 21 minutes 6 seconds in 1979, but his record was broken frequently by Craig Ferguson, who won a total of ten races between 1985 and 1997 and whose best time, 20 minutes 34 seconds, remains unbroken. Other winners of the men's race have been Keith Campbell, Niall Bennie (twice), Goff Todd, Ian Prescott (twice), Craig Tweedie, and Jock Jackson (twice).

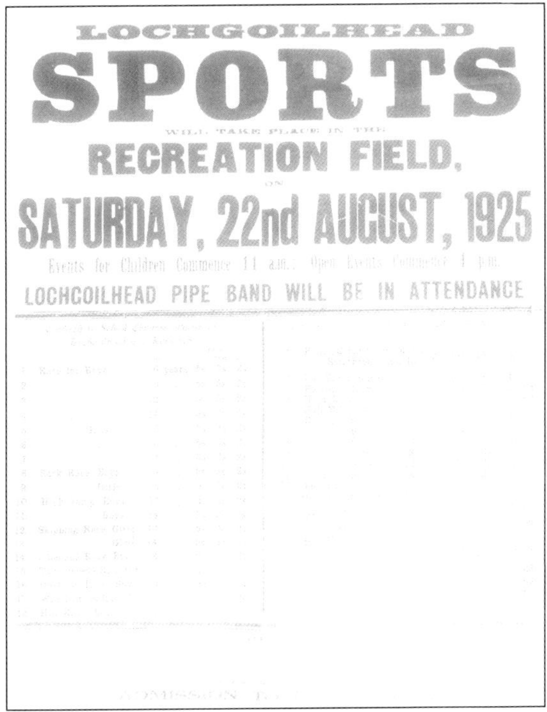

5.17 The programme for sports' day, 1925

A race for the ladies, to the little Steeple, was started in 1981, when Alison Coghill set a time of 19 minutes 38 seconds. Alison also won the following two years, but the greatest number of wins is held by Linda Leyland, who was successful five times with a personal best of 16 minutes 37 seconds. The record is held by Marie Todd, who won twice in two incredibly fast times – 16 minutes 3 seconds in 1985 and 13 minutes 36 seconds in 1987. Other winners have been Lou Todd, Debbie Hammon (twice), Katie Broadbent, Marie Brodie, Marie Templeton, Kate Thoms and Fiona Mathie.

In 2000 – the fortieth anniversary – the veterans' trophies were introduced, one each for men and women. Veterans were defined as ladies aged 35 and over and men aged 40 and over. The hill race had to be abandoned in 2001 on account of the precautions taken to prevent foot and mouth disease spreading to the area.

5.16 The day of Willie MacNicol's retirement, 1977:
1 Andy Hammon, 2 Liza Brown, 4 Mrs Ross, 6 Grace Scott, 7 Alistair Urquhart, 8 Davy MacLachlan, 9 Jean Campbell, 10 Daisy MacLachlan, 11 Douglas Campbell, 12 Willie MacNicol, 13 Eric Carroll, 14 Lena Carroll, 15 Onie Scott, 16 Maggie Brodie, 20 Elaine Carroll, 22 Frankie Baker, 23 Allan Campbell, 24 Calum MacDonald, 25 Jimmy MacGready, 26 Eddie Stewart, 27 Hazel Henderson, 28 Catriona MacInnes, 30 Willie MacDougall, 31 Nancy Hammon, 32 Calum MacInnes, 33 Shona Cushley, 34 Helena Cannon, 35 Sheena Campbell, 36 Heather MacInnes, 40 Liz MacNicol, 43 Fraser Boyd, 44 Neil Bennie, 45 Roy Campbell, 47 Nicky Endicott, 48 Debbie Hammon, 49 Anne Carroll, 50 Wendy Hammon

Willie MacNicol

Willie MacNicol, who lived in Pier Brae, drove the Lochgoilhead bus every day for thirty-one years. He was actually born in Dalmally, in June 1910, and it was only after his army service, around 1946, that he moved to Lochgoil and began driving the bus for David MacBrayne. When the service was taken over by Western SMT the company thought that Willie was too valuable a man to lose, and he drove for them for four years. Then the service was taken over by Douglas Campbell, and Willie remained as driver until his retirement in 1977 at the age of sixty-seven. When he arrived back in the village on his last trip there was a surprise reception waiting for him: the locals had all turned out to greet him, and a ceilidh and presentation had been organised in the village hall. Willie was presented with a tankard by Allison Harper on behalf of all the Dunoon Grammar School pupils, and he also received a rose bowl and a wallet, as well as gifts from Lochgoilhead Hotel and Carrick Castle Hotel. The festivities went on until after 2 a.m.

Lochgoil Silver Jubilee Celebrations

In June 1977 Lochgoil held four days of celebrations in honour of the queen's silver jubilee. The planned events started with a cabaret, supper and dance at Carrick Castle Hotel on the evening of Friday 3rd; incorporated on the Saturday a coffee morning at the village hall, a gymkhana at Corrow, a whist and beetle drive at the school, and a barbecue and bonfire (with pop music) at the gravel pit; continued on the Sunday with a special morning service at the church, a children's regatta at Carrick and a power-boat handicap race at Inverlounin; and culminated on the Monday with fancy dress, sports and highland games and, finally, a dance in the village hall. The *Loch Goil Jubilee Bulletin*, hand-produced by Eric Carroll, reports in rhyme:

Twenty days of sunshine
In a hot unbroken run
And then – it rains on Saturday.
What had you sinners done?

Wait! I have not finished
I've another verse for you
To tell you that on Sunday
The wind it really blew.

We had to cancel boating.
But another day we'll try,
So get your dinghies ready
For the second of July.

The opening dance was a sell-out, and the Silver Jubilee Queen, Deanna Bailey, was chosen. The gymkhana took place despite the rain on Saturday, and the bulletin reports that the horses behaved well – most of the time. The barbecue, however, was wisely transferred to the indoor riding school, where there was "a memorable evening of pop, smoke, noise and enthusiasm". As for the bonfire, "it may not have been the biggest in Britain, but few can have burned more gloriously in rain than ours did." For Monday, the Big Day, conditions again made outdoor activities impossible: "Time was short, and the village went into action under full throttle. The police, in the interests of avoidance of any possible civil disturbance, drove round the village announcing by loud-hailer that the venue had been changed. The decorators of the village hall moved their flags to the riding school, and numerous young men moved the etceteras from the floor of the riding school to somewhere else. Sandy Mackenzie forgot his shop and became a transporter of furniture and tea equipment. Rain fell and snow whitened Ben Donich." As for the final dance, "it was fun, it was crowded, it was happy ... and the Post Office the next morning did not seem to be quite itself."

The Hi-Jack

Up until 1992 the Royal Bank of Scotland provided a weekly banking service in the village hall, but one day in August or September that year, as the two lady bankers drove up Hell's Glen, they were held up, bundled into the back

5.18 Moses' Well and Hell's Glen at a time when highway robbery would have required a horse for a quick getaway; this postcard, dated 4 August 1906, bears the message "Very wet"!

of a van and abducted with the day's takings. Two very shaken ladies were later found at the roadside at Loch Lomond. Not surprisingly, the bank then suspended the service, leaving everyone with a journey into Inveraray or Dunoon to see their friendly bank manager. Fortunately for all, in summer 2004 the Royal Bank of Scotland introduced its new mobile banking service to the village.

The Rise and Fall of Hollywood in the Goil

During the Second World War Drimsynie was owned by Mrs Isabella Grove. She was a film distributor and was therefore able to give Lochgoilhead residents previews of the latest films before they made it to the main cinemas. The Land Army girls stationed at Blair Lomond were among the viewers. Starting in the 1940s and continuing into the 1960s, when television found its way into most homes, the Highlands and Islands Film Guild regularly showed films in the village hall. It was common practice to bring along a cushion, as the wooden benches proved a bit uncomfortable.

During the 1970s, while the film *From Russia with Love* was being made (partly on location in Scotland), the star, Sean Connery, came to Lochgoilhead in an effort to find some solitude for a weekend break. He arrived on a Friday evening – in secret, as he thought – but by Saturday morning hundreds of people had descended on the village. As a result he cut short his "relaxing break" and was assisted in leaving the village clandestinely.

5.19 Sean Connery taking time off in Lochgoilhead during the shooting of "From Russia with Love", 1970s

The next "memorable" occasion was the visit of Sidney Devine to record a programme that was shot to a great extent in front of the Shore House. Sidney could be heard warbling across the loch. This may not have done much for the village!

The first film for the silver screen to make use of the now famous location was *Restless Natives*. Two unknown young actors, the Scot Robert Urquhart and the American Ned Beatty, were ably supported by locals Jackie Boyd, Tom Murray, Nancy Hammon, Derek Prescott, Johnny Liddell and Simon Hunter. Our old and much-loved bus driver Willie MacNicol drove an old MacBraynes bus, which was central to the story.

In 1994 Judith Chalmers visited Drimsynie to film the television programme "Wish You Were Here". The highlight of this was a dinner dance, when the locals were invited at a subsidised rate to act as guests dancing quaint Scottish dances to a ceilidh band. As we recollect, Judith was very complimentary about Lochgoilhead, if not the dancing.

There followed an excellent series of children's programmes on the outdoors for BBC2 called "Fully Booked", presented by Zoe Ball and Grant Stott. Lochgoilhead appeared in the "Buried Treasure" section with the active assistance of Sam Tweedlie and his team at the Lochgoilhead Centre.

Over the winter of 1998–9 *My Life So Far* was filmed at Cairndow, creating temporary and remunerative employment for many of our restless natives, among them the curling virtuosi Mike Dimmer, Len Gow and Alex Burgess, as well as George Dempster and Mike Watts, among others. Mark Evans was cast in a particularly important part when he was promoted to fill in for the tramp, who evidently had a more important engagement elsewhere. It took Mark about two hours to be made up for the role, which involved his being "buried alive" in a pile of leaves.

Back in the village, around the same time the excellent novel *The Crow Road* by Iain Banks was filmed in typical Lochgoilhead weather (pouring). The action took place around the post office and the Blacks' house, Cruachan, which was posing as a dentist's surgery, and featured Andy and Dean Hammon and a cameo role for Junior MacPherson.

Finally, following a pilot episode in 1999, the BBC television series "Brotherly Love" returned in 2000 to give more village thespians delusions of grandeur. The entire primary school featured in one episode, while another involved a scene in the church, when some unaccustomed faces appeared in the congregation.

The Cannon of Battery Point

The two cannon at Battery Point were first mounted during the Napoleonic Wars, which would put the date of their installation between 1795 and 1810, at least one hundred years before the present house was built. The point where they were mounted commands a view right down to Carrick Castle, so it is easy to see why the site was chosen. Rumour has it that they vanished for scrap during the Second World War, but that is untrue, for two reliable witnesses saw them in position in 1953; the same witnesses heard that they had later been tipped over the wall into the sea to discourage sightseers from climbing the wall to examine them. This story would also appear to be doubtful, as at least one came to light around 1995 and is almost certainly still in existence.

That year a member of the Rifle Club received a Christmas card showing a picture, complete with history, of one of the cannon which "used to be mounted at Battery Point, Lochgoilhead". It was an obvious 6 pounder, mounted on a standard artillery carriage. The card was duly passed to the present owner as a matter of interest, and enquiries revealed that the cannon was then mounted in the garden of the sender's father, who lived at Eaglesham. A subsequent visit to the house found no trace, and no sender's father; it transpired that during the enquiries, which had taken several months, the father had died and the cannon had been sold on. Regrettably once again the trail went cold.

Somewhere out there is at least one, if not both, of the original cannon, and if anyone should become aware of their present location it would be nice to see them restored to their ancient position in Argyll!

Animal Corner

In the 1940s John Neilson, who as a teenager lived at Corriesyke House (now the Naval Base), caught a deer on the opposite side of the loch. He had no transport to carry it home, but since it was a still night he shouted across the water, hoping his family might hear him. They didn't, but a navy boat, which was in the loch at the time, did and collected both him and the deer and carried them across. His mother and brothers hung the carcass in the garage and as a thank you to the navy shared the venison with them.

***

Captain and Mrs Watson lived at Burnknowe. Mrs Watson, who was French, was a very large lady. Because of her size she found the walk to the village daunting, so she kept a donkey in the garden and would ride it to the village with a pannier for her shopping. On occasions she would collect heather, put it in the pannier and sell it in the village to raise money for charity.

***

Bash Blair, who maintained that his family had been in Lochgoilhead since the days of Robert the Bruce, kept cows and sold milk at his byre along Inverlounin Road. His cows were infamous: they were recognised by name by the villagers as they strolled the streets. One in particular, called Annie Borthwick, learned to open gates and caused havoc in the gardens, destroying flowers and vegetables. Fruit and vegetables displayed outside the local shop were not safe either when Annie was about. Apparently on one occasion, tempted by the smell of fresh nesting hay, she managed to squeeze herself into a hen house. Unfortunately for the owner of the shed she got stuck and was unable to turn around, so the only solution was to dismantle the shed around her.

Among the other favourite cows whose names are remembered were Bunty, Baldie, Whitie, Elmer, Stumpy, Hilda and Agnes. Local children

5.21 Bash Blair, 1950s

would wait at the byre at milking times for a drink of warm milk. By the door of the byre was a large barrel of molasses. While the children were waiting for the milk Bash would dip a stick into the barrel and give it to them to lick. This was considered a special treat.

One year Bash kept his bull in the byre all winter. Naturally the manure accumulated, and when spring came he found he couldn't get the door open to let the bull out until the manure had been dug down to ground level again.

As well as the tame beasts wandering around Lochgoil, Bash Blair was responsible for a herd of cattle roaming the hills behind the village. These cattle had been left to their own devices for many years, and because of interbreeding and lack of contact with humans had become wild. It was only because of new government legislation in the early 1950s requiring that all cattle be tested for TB that the question arose of how to round them up. It was decided that, apart from asking for local volunteers, assistance should be sought from the crew of the destroyer HMS *Savage*, which was in Loch Goil for trials. It was obvious that some of the cattle, too dangerous to be rounded up, would have to be shot, and some of the navy personnel were experienced with guns.

Those cattle which could be rounded up were herded into a fank behind the village. The next step was to transfer them into a wooden float. However, once the doors were closed the cramped conditions caused them to panic, and the decision was taken, as the float began to disintegrate, to open the doors. Like in a scene from a wild west movie, the cattle stampeded through the village, and sailors and volunteers could be seen running in all directions to avoid being mowed down. Doors were firmly closed behind small children as the stampeding cattle dashed like lemmings towards the pier. The owner of Fulton's Stores, keen to get a safe view of the momentous occasion, was seen to clamber up onto the corrugated iron roof of his shop. When the cattle reached the pier they rushed into the loch and swam all the way across to the other side, a distance of about three-quarters of a mile. The surviving cattle were eventually tested and found to be free of the disease, but this incident meant that Argyll was one of the last counties – if not the last – to be declared free.

***

For many years there have been swans on the loch, and pairs have nested on the glebe at the mouth of the River Goil. This land is prone to flooding by the equinoctial tides, and villagers were constantly having to rescue the eggs before the cold water spoilt them. In the 1950s Duncan Henderson, who lived with his parents at the courtyard at Drimsynie, constructed a raised nest for the swans in order to keep them above the flood level, and cygnets were hatched regularly. One year, however, his father came home and told him that the nest was about to be flooded so, while his mother kept the birds at bay with a broom, Duncan retrieved the eggs, took them home and put them in the family's warming oven. Once the flood had subsided he returned the eggs to the nest and the female swan happily resumed sitting. Her brood was safely hatched. Duncan was later interviewed by the press, who made quite a story about the swans "Jack and Jenny".

In the 1970s Derek Prescott built and anchored a raft onto which he moved the swans' nest, so that when the flood came the nest floated and the eggs were safe. Somehow the BBC heard of this and in 1983 featured the story on the television programme "Wildtrack".

While a pair of swans has remained a feature of the loch, cygnets seem to be a rarer phenomenon, though in June 2001 three were produced. In 2003 the swans were joined by a gaggle of four geese, who are now a familiar sight.

***

Not that long ago patrons would go into the bar of the Lochgoilhead Hotel with their dogs, on the slim pretext that they were out walking said mutts. On several occasions one of the dog owners (who will remain nameless as he is still a pillar of village society) received a call from the landlord to say that he had gone home of a Saturday "lunchtime" and had left his dog behind. Unfortunately at some point Norman White's Great Dane took a bite out of a customer, and thereafter dogs were banned.

***

In the late 1980s Jack Revie, then the officer in charge of the Naval Base, lived in Cove. He commuted each day in a red mini. One winter's morning on his way to work he noticed something fall from the telephone wires beside the road in Gleann Mor. When he stopped to investigate he found it was a buzzard that was completely encased in ice. Presuming the bird to be dead he put it in the boot of his car and took it with him to the base. After he arrived he opened the boot to show some of his staff, and to their surprise they found that the bird wasn't dead after all. The ice had begun to melt a little. They decided to put the buzzard in a warm shed that was used by a visiting team of divers. A few hours later they looked in the window to see how the bird was getting on, only to find a rather large and now very angry buzzard. At this point some argument ensued as to who should let it out. Eventually a way of releasing it from a safe distance was devised, and the bird flew off, apparently none the worse for its journey in the boot of the red mini.

Chapter Six

Lochgoil during the War Years

There can have been few towns and villages unaffected by the two world wars of the twentieth century. The Lochgoil area was no exception: the war memorial carries the names of sixteen young men killed in the Great War and four – the postman's son, the minister's son, the stepson of the "laird" and the son of a widow of the First World War – who lost their lives between 1939 and 1945. In the village hall there are framed rolls of honour, listing the names of all those who served in both conflicts.

Local men also served in the Boer War in South Africa (1899–1902), and the son of the Revd McCorkindale, John, was a casualty of the siege of Mafeking, being killed on 6 April 1900 at the age of 26. When it was over the lads who had fought came back on the paddle steamer *Windsor Castle*. They marched from the pierhead to the grassy area in front of Callander Cottage. All the schoolchildren, among them Annie Cameron (the grandmother of Hugh Cameron-White), lined the route, waving small flags and singing a patriotic jingle of the time, "Piper Findlay", to the tune of "Cock of the North": "He sat for oors and frightened the Boers and won the Victoria Cross."

The First World War

It is not difficult to imagine the effect of the losses in the war of 1914–18 on the small and close-knit communities of the time. The following excerpts from Lochgoilhead and Kilmorich Parish Magazine, written by the Revd D. M. Maclean, show that those left at home were closely involved with the war effort.

December 1917

We were very glad to see recently, home on leave from France, Archibald Haggart, who has won the Military Medal for conspicuous gallantry on the field – he repeatedly carried despatches through heavy "curtain fire". His mother has good reason to be proud of him, and we offer them both our heartiest congratulations.

John Johnston and Donald Fraser were also home on leave and both looking fit. Robert Mitchell and Hugh Clark, both wounded in the spring offensive, were again sent to France, but the latter has been wounded again and is now in England. We hope to see him back before long in Lochgoilhead, where his native air will soon set him up again.

Archibald Sinclair and Robert McInnes were both suffering from shell shock in France. The former is again in the firing line. Archibald Blair and his cousin Malcolm (of Carrick Farm) are both in France, and word has recently come of Joseph Clark's safe arrival in Mesopotamia. Donald Maclachlan, Inveronich, and his cousin Ian (Lochwood) are both serving in the same reserve battalion in this country.

We are pleased to record that William Armstrong, who was invalided home from East Africa, where he had served for a considerable time, has been posted to a military instructorship at Bedford. His younger brother, James, who served in France with the "Eighth", has almost completed his course of instruction at the Cadet School with a view to a commission.

Intimation has just been received that Lieutenant John Taylor, Lettermay, serving with the forces in Palestine, was wounded in the recent offensive. Details are not yet to hand of the extent of his injuries, but we earnestly hope for reassuring news of him, and we offer our sympathy to his parents and sister during their anxious hours of suspense.

Quite a number of our Kilmorich lads have been home on leave.

Donald McGillivray was very seriously wounded by shrapnel, but when we last saw him he was well on the road to recovery. He is now in Ireland. His brother Angus was called up in July. Winton Galloway was also severely wounded, but was detained in France during convalescence. He has now rejoined his unit. The following were among those home on leave: Thomas Galloway and Hugh McKellar, both of the Canadians, the latter on sick leave, and A. McMaster.

We are glad to see Mr Nicol Luke, Elder, in our midst again. Under the recent regulation he has been released from military service for a period of three months in order to engage in work of military importance.

These all with the rest of our boys who are now on service are bearing their share of the common burden. And what of those of us whose lot it is to tarry by the stuff? The authorities are daily impressing upon us – what indeed our unaided conscience should tell us with equal insistence – that our own hearty cooperation is necessary in order that the labours and sacrifices of our brave boys may not be in vain.

wounded, this time severely with shrapnel in the hand. Notwithstanding every care in an English hospital, he never properly recovered, and after pneumonia set in he succumbed on 30th January.

His body was sent home for burial, and there was a large gathering of mourners to pay their last respects. The local Company of the Argyllshire Volunteers under Major Macfarlane and Sergt David MacLachlan turned out. After a short service at the house, the cortege, headed by Piper McPhail and the Volunteers, proceeded to the parish church. There a public service was conducted by the minister, Rev. D. M. Maclean, M.A., and the Rev. J. McK. Campbell, M.A., of the United Free Church. As the mourners left the church, Miss Hall, organist, played "The Dead March" in "Saul". After consigning the remains to earth, three volleys were fired over the grave by the Volunteers. The whole proceedings were solemn and impressive. Private Clark was 24 years of age, and was employed in the Forestry Department of Glasgow Corporation. He was of a quiet, unassuming character, and liked by all with whom he came into contact. The sympathy of the whole district goes out to Mr and Mrs Clark and family.

***

A LOCHGOILHEAD HERO

Private W. Fraser, A&S Highlanders

General regret has been expressed at the death of Private William Fraser, Argyll and Sutherland Highlanders, who died a hero's death from wounds received in the advance on 13th November. The following letter from a comrade has been received by Private Fraser's sister:

Just a little note of sympathy for you all from Willie's old section. I cannot tell you how sorry we all are, and the boys have asked me to write to you expressing their sorrow. We lost a lot of chaps that morning, but none we miss more than Willie. He was wounded at the German first line when we attacked. I was not with him at the time, but came across him a few minutes later. He was badly hit, but was his usual quiet self, and talked to us while we dressed him. We immediately took him back to our own line, and sent him on to the dressing station. I had to leave him then, and was very sorry to hear the sad news of his death. We all mourn the loss of a good comrade and a brave soldier.

***

William Fraser, who received his fatal wounds at Beaumont Hamel, is also buried in Lochgoilhead churchyard, as is Archibald Blair, the son of James and Catherine Blair of Alma, who died in the military hospital *Edinburgh Castle* on 14 November 1918 at the age of 26. Many more of course were buried where they fell. The gravestone of John (*d* 1946) and Catherine (*d* 1964) Campbell tells a sad story, as one of their sons, Norman, died on 20 March 1910 aged nine, a second son, John, was killed in France on 17 March 1917 aged 20, and a third, Alexander, was lost at sea on 14 July 1942 at the age of 34. And the Revd Maclean's son, Hayward Gillian Carruthers Maclean, who was born in 1911 and would therefore have had childhood memories of the Great War, was killed in action in 1940. His grave "is a soldier's known unto God, in France".

Memories of the 1940s

In the twenty-first century there are, of course, still people in the village, or who grew up in the village, who have memories of the years of the Second World War. Hugh Neilson remembers the day war was declared:

> *We as a family (seven of us) were at church, and it was conducted by the Rev. Dan Maclean. He made the announcement from the pulpit. All was despair and despondency because those who were old enough, and most of them were, remembered the First World War and all that it entailed.*
>
> *Talk of a German invasion was often discussed, and one of the first signs of an invasion would be the ringing of the church bells throughout the country. One particularly peaceful day not long after the beginning of the war Lochgoilhead church bells were to be*

Next door but one from Craigenreoch, Dr Stalker at Drynan (now The Peel House) had three evacuees from the Channel Islands (which were, of course, occupied by the Germans) staying with her for the duration of the war – Mrs Woolie, Grace Gerard and Dr Macgregor. While the two women went home after the war, Dr Macgregor so fell in love with Scotland that he chose to remain.

6.3 Lochgoil's nurses during the Second World War (back row, left to right): Catriona Maclean, Myra Cowan, Catriona McNeilage, Ina Cameron, Lily Cowan, Jean Urquhart, Winifred MacFarlane; (front row) Nancy Munro, Mrs Neilson, Henrietta Forman, Hattie MacFarlane, Mrs Hall, Nan Leslie

***

Hugh Cameron-White remembers particularly the fact that food was rationed, and that there were Land Army girls in the village, wearing their very distinctive uniform of hat, dark green top and fawn twill trousers. Johnnie Weir the butcher acquired some whale meat which you could buy without ration books, and Dougie Cameron and his brother Colin went out fishing one day and gave his mother some slaithe; she came out in big red spots after eating it! She used to cook on the fire or by primus stove: one day the jet on the primus got blocked and they had none of the prickers required to clear the blockage, but fortunately some cyclists in the village came to the rescue. Decent cigarettes were difficult to get, but the butcher also sold cigarettes and Mrs Weir used to give his mother the nod when some were coming in.

People would come in the boat and stay for a few days, so the arrival of the Comet at the pier was a big occasion each day, and the children always went down to see the folk coming ashore. Grace McEwan collected the pier dues in her wee hut at the shore end of the pier. There were no favourites: everyone had to pay.

There were a lot of seamen from ships which used to come to the loch for various reasons, and quite a few of the local girls – including Cathie Armstrong and Tilly MacLachlan – procured husbands as a result. Tilly's wedding reception was held in the village hall, where Walter MacCallum played the pipes and Hugh's mother, Margaret Cameron, danced the highland fling.

***

Cathie Armstrong met her husband, Neil MacDonald, when she was only 17. Neil was a crewman on one of the many merchant ships that had been, or was waiting to go, on convoy in the Atlantic with its cargo of ammunition. Ships would lie comparatively safely at anchor in the shelter of the loch, but there would have been quite some explosion if there had been any kind of accident! Cathie was married in 1948, and Grace McEwan was her bridesmaid. She remembers that people were very used to making their own entertainment in the 1940s. During the war years there was evidently a flourishing badminton club with the visiting seamen taking part, and the Women's Rural, formed in 1947, regularly put on plays and pantomimes.

***

Duncan Henderson recalled that there was a light railway by Glaslet Bridge from the sawmill at Drimsynie to carry the timber that had been felled down to the lochside. It was then taken away by puffer to be used in the war effort. The mass forestry plantations that are so familiar nowadays were, of course still in the future, and before the 1950s sheep were grazed all the way down the glen from the Rest. The 1920 Ordnance Survey map of Lochgoilhead shows the area of larches that provided the timber. (In 1953 this was the first area to be replanted after the war, and was known as the Coronation plantation.) There was also another sawmill and stables on the old road used by the Land Girls.

renovation and redecoration. Meanwhile the congregation has been holding their services in the church hall.

Originally dedicated as "the Church of the Three Holy Brethren", the present building, in the words of the Revd J. H. Kerr, minister of the parish, is a place of venerable antiquity. Evidence of its first dedication has been found in the Vatican registers of present in Papal register of appointments to the charge, and in Papal calendars, but the identity of the three brethren is still unknown.

IRISH KING

One theory, which had the support of the late Duke of Argyll, is that the brethren were the sons of an early Irish king. After considerable research he came to the conclusion that they were the three sons of Nessan, who was descended in the eleventh generation from Cathair Mor, king of Ireland from 174 AD to 177 AD.

There has also been much speculation as to whether the brethren were the three brothers of Our Lord or the Three Wise Men from the East, to whom there were many dedications on the Continent.

Within the church the principal features of historical importance are mainly contained in the east–west block, which probably represents the extent of the medieval church. At the end of the north wall, for instance, there is the chantry-altar to Our Lady, and on the east gable itself there stands an elaborate Renaissance monument.

THREE CORBELS

The chantry-altar was founded in 1512 by Ian Campbell, the fourth Laird of Ardkinglas, and is surmounted by an arched monument with three carved niche-heads and three corbels. Two of the corbels carry the armorial bearings of Campbell and those of his father-in-law, Walter Buchanan, fifteenth laird of that ilk. The third corbel is defaced. Presumably it once bore some religious device, perhaps the monogram of the Virgin Mary.

Symbols on the base of the shrine resemble articles such as scissors and have led a number of people to suppose that a seamstress, possibly a nun, was interred there. Mr Kerr, however, rejects this theory. He takes the view that the characters are more likely to be symbolic of rural life and crafts.

BURIAL VAULT

The monument on the east wall bears the Campbell coat of arms and apparently commemorates the ninth laird, who was declared forfeit at the cross of Edinburgh in 1662. Designed as an architectural surround to a small doorway giving access to a burial vault, where the male descendants of the Ardkinglas Campbells were laid to rest, it is at least 20ft high and about 12ft broad at the base. The vault was demolished in 1849 and the doorway is now built up.

Another link with the past, and one that is as yet unfamiliar to the congregation, is the installation of an imposing sounding-box type pulpit, which has been received from the kirk session of the disused church of Kiltearn, Easter Ross. This pulpit is said to have been occupied by the Revd Thomas Hog, a notable preacher in the middle of the sixteenth century. It has been placed on a dais in the central area of the church and faces the north aisle, which was built in the eighteenth century. A precentor's box attached to the pulpit has been retained as a reading-desk.

GLASS REPLACED

The work of restoration has included the cleaning and repairing of the antiquities and the redecorating of their inscriptions and heraldic bearings. Numerous repairs have been done to the structure of the building, notably the replacement of coloured glass in the four main windows in the south wall with clear-glass astragal windows in keeping with the period of the main fabric; the provision of an organ and choir loft; and the installation of improved systems of heating and lighting, the latter fittings being reproductions of seventeenth-century Dutch-type chandeliers. The church has also been redecorated and its soft furnishings renewed.

Iain G. Lindsay and Partners, Edinburgh, were the architects.

DIRECT APPEAL

Financial assistance has been given by the Pilgrim Trust, the Baird Trust, and the Church and Manse Committee of the Home Board of the Church of Scotland, but by far the major share of the cost has been met by the congregation. Although the total roll is only 186 they have contributed more than £3000 in the past two years for the church fabric of the parish.

The Portincaple Rail Link

On Friday 18 December 1896 a meeting was held in the school at Lochgoilhead "for the purpose of considering what steps should be taken to further the action of the Carrick Castle feuars and other in connection with the proposed Portincaple New Railway Scheme."

Duncan McKellar, who was a builder in Lochgoilhead at that time, called the meeting, and among those present there were "Revd McCorkindale, Revd Jas. Campbell, Dr. R. J. Halliday, and Messrs. Lewis McFarlane of *Invermay* [the house which is now Ardroy, Fife Council's outdoor centre]; Donald McArthur of *Kilvaree* [the house at the base, Douglas Pier]; Wm. Smith, *Schoolhouse*; Geo. Adams, *Margowan*; Andrew Blair, *Oakburn*; Jas. Blair, contractor; Donald Fraser; Jas. B. Stewart, of the Carrick Castle committee; Mr. Carstairs C.A. factor for Glenfinart Estates and others."

In essence, the purpose of this meeting, and those which followed, was to establish a steamer or ferry link with Portincaple and a bus service to the West Highland Railway line at Whistlefied station. (Hector Blair ran a motorboat ferry service to Portincaple carrying 12 passengers.) A similar proposal had been put forward in 1893 which had not been adopted, and there seemed some doubts as to the viability of reviving the scheme. However, it was decided to appoint a deputation to approach the railway

8.7 James Blair with the Revd Campbell (centre) and the Revd McCorkindale (seated, right)

company and request that further consideration should be given to the proposal.

Action on the matter seems to have been fairly rapid, as an informal meeting of those appointed to be part of the deputation met the following day to discuss a plan of action. Within a few days (22 December) a meeting took place in the Glasgow office of Mr J. M. Taylor, who had been involved with the 1893 scheme. He expressed considerable uncertainty on the wisdom of reopening the project and suggested that the formation of such a deputation was, indeed, futile. However, as the deputation had been assembled, moves were made to arrange meetings with managers of the Glasgow and South Western Railway Company and the marine superintendent, Captain Williamson, and this was eventually arranged with Mr F. H. Gillies of the railway company. Their request was basically for improved services to and from Loch Goil, especially at weekends and in the winter months. Approaches were also made to the West Highland Railway Company and the Loch Goil Steamboat Company.

8.8 Robert Fraser (a relative of the Blairs) discussing a proposed trip down the loch, 1905; in those days everyone dressed in their best clothes for such occasions

8.9 A steamer arriving at the pier, 1950s

the villagers and regularly competed in football matches. They also attended all the dances and were often guests in people's homes.

One summer in the 1950s a French submarine visited Loch Goil. During its stay the crew got to know the locals and were delighted at the friendliness and hospitality shown to them. Shortly before their departure they made a strange request, for roses and empty bottles. The ladies of the village were delighted with the bottles of rosewater that resulted, given as a token of thanks.

"Scotland's Grand Old Lady of the Sea"

Ardroy was the one-time home of Lita Edwards, known to many as "Captain Jimmy Edwards". The *Daily Record* of 24 August 1973 honoured her with a full-page article after, at the age of 73, she and her novice crew of sea scouts and a sea guide had finished seventh out of sixteen starters in the 110-mile Coca-Cola race for tall ships (four didn't finish). The race had taken 32 hours and the captain had had only four hours' sleep during that time. At that point she was Scotland's oldest yacht skipper and master mariner, and showed no signs of growing old on dry land.

Lita Edwards fell in love with sailing when her father bought her a small dinghy for her fourteenth birthday. During the Second World War she was a petty-officer small boat skipper in the WRENS, and her job was to take ships up to the size of a tank landing craft into the harbours around Southampton Water for the build-up to D-Day and afterwards. Needless to say, there were several commanders who were unhappy about handing over their ship to a woman! After the war Miss Edwards decided to operate her own boat yard, and found the ideal spot at Lochgoilhead. In 1950 she bought her 52 foot cedar and mahogany ketch in Ireland for the bargain price (because of her poor condition) of £700 – the cost of the 6 tons of lead on her keel – and named her *Sibyl of Cumae* after the wisest of the sibyls in classical mythology. When she was launched in 1902 the boat took eight strong men to race her, so Miss Edwards altered her so that she would be easily handled by a young crew. For many years she taught seamanship as a voluntary helper at the Scout Centre, and there must be several hundred scouts who learned to sail with this most unusual skipper.

Chapter Nine
Memories

In any community there are tales to be heard from those who have spent much or all of their lives within that community. Sadly, many of these stories are never recorded, and with the passing on of these people a wealth of memories and history disappears.

Davy MacLachlan

Davy MacLachlan (1909–1997) devoted a great deal of time researching the history and culture of the village and attempted to document all the Gaelic names of the area. In the notes he left he outlined his love for the area, and how he felt a warmth and friendship in the hills and glens around him. He regretted the loss of the old people and the old ways.

The Duke's Path and Argyll's Bowling Green

This ancient path was a bridle track used by travellers as a shortcut from the Lowlands into the Highlands. It may well have been exploited by monks travelling from Paisley Abbey to the Church of the Three Brethren in Lochgoilhead. The Campbells would certainly have used it as a faster way to reach Glasgow than the longer route over the pass of the Rest and Be Thankful (as it later came to be known). It is possible that this was also a safer route, as it passed through Campbell country rather than the potentially hazardous MacFarlane lands around Arrochar and the MacGregor lands across Loch Lomond. Whether the duke himself actually used the route is debatable, but it is thought that he may have done so on occasion.

Although the original path fell into disuse and parts are now difficult to trace, in 2002–3 the Forestry Commission undertook a lot of work restoring the early sections, from opposite Invermay on Inverlounin Road up to the forest track and then up through the woods to new bridges over the Inverlounin burn (*Allt Inverlounin*) and the *Allt Garbh* burn. Past the Stuckbeg

9.2 Volunteer helpers for the Glasgow Corporation picnic pose outside the village hall, 1930s; the picnic, for underprivileged children from the city, took place annually in May until shortly before the Second World War

Inveronich was mentioned in the Cowal valuation of 1791, when its value was more than that of Drimsynie, Correw [Corrow] or Polchorktan [Pole Farm].

Later several properties in Lochgoil came under the ownership of Glasgow Corporation. Inveronich was among these, and was rented out to tenants. At one time during the war years there were five families housed there, and sadly and bizarrely each family lost the eldest son in battle.

Adjacent to Donich Lodge, an impressive building which in its heyday was a shooting lodge, there was a bridge that was closed one day every year to prevent its becoming a right of way. The remains of this bridge are clearly visible a few yards upstream of the present Forestry Enterprise bridge. A new bungalow, also called Donich Lodge, was built near the bridge in 2002.

In 1957 the Forestry Commission received a special rush order from Glasgow Corporation. It was critical that the deadline be met, but there was one problem: the horses and wagons needed to transport the felled trees weren't able to reach the location at the Meeting of the Waters. It was decided that the forestry workers would have to take on the task themselves. Every available man was hired, and they worked round the clock, felling and dragging the huge trunks to where they could be uplifted, knowing that they were going to earn huge bonuses for their efforts. The felled trees lie there to this day ... waiting to be collected?

9.3 Before the arrival of articulated timber lorries, forestry workers relied on horses and carts to move huge tree trunks; this photograph dates from 1927

What is now known as the Nursery was in the first half of the twentieth century a source of a variety of vegetables grown by the two full-time gardeners of Inveronich estate. For one shilling [5p] one could have a pail filled to the brim with potatoes, carrots, turnips, etc., always topped with a bunch of fresh parsley.

9.4 Haymaking at the Nursery; David McCallum is on the far right

Campbell's Leap

At one time a Campbell occupant of Corran Bay returned home to find his home being ransacked by redcoats. In his anger he attacked one of the soldiers, striking him a heavy blow with a stout stick. He soon realised the folly of such an attack and fled from the scene along the beach. A passing boat saw his predicament and came near to the shore, enabling Campbell to jump to the boat and escape capture. The place is marked on maps as *Leum Chaimbeulaich* ("Campbell's Leap").

The '45

During the 1745 Jacobite rising the people of this area were divided by their allegiances. The Campbells of Argyll and their followers were supporters of George II and the government, while many of the Highland clans supported James Stuart exiled in France.

In November 1745 news reached Inveraray that some of Prince Charles's Jacobite forces, under Gregor MacGregor of Glengyle (a nephew of Rob Roy), were to engage in a recruiting campaign to rally support for the prince. His intention was to make for Castle Lachlan, where he hoped to be met by other supporters. However, in passing through Lochgoilhead, MacGregor talked too freely, revealing his plans, and was overheard by Duncan Campbell. Campbell contacted Inveraray with details of the conversation, and companies of Louden's regiment were dispatched from Inveraray to dispel the gathering. During the skirmish Glengyle was forced to retreat and lost two men, with fourteen wounded and a further twenty-one taken prisoner. Just one was killed from the Louden regiment.

The Legend of Beach (Beoch)

The old farm of Beach (formerly Beoch) gets its name from a legend dating back to 1510, when an old chronicler related that a strange beast (*beoch*) came from the "pool of Argyle". It was recorded that by a mere wag of its tail it struck down oak trees and so alarmed the inhabitants that they banded themselves together to attack it. The beast retaliated with a further wag of its tail, killing three men. The remainder fled for safety to the highest tree tops. At this point the monster returned to the deep waters of the loch, never to be seen again! It was reported that the beast was web-footed.

***

LOCH GOIL

by Davy MacLachlan, 1964

On the side of the brae
Where the lambkins play,
And the shepherd comes home from his toil,
The breeze from the west,
It has gone to its rest:
'Tis springtime in Lochgoil.

On the mountain steep
Where the angels sleep,
And the sunset's rays recoil,
One can see at a glance
Where the fairies dance:
'Tis summer in Lochgoil.

9.7 Alec McEwan standing outside Jackson's stores; Walter MacCallum is at the wheel of the car

Grace also sold the Sunday papers from the green sheds (the shops being closed on Sundays). These were set out either on a trestle table or on the bonnet of her green A35 van. She provided papers to order for established customers only and not for passing trade, and her order with the supplier was very well defined, so it was difficult to change your paper. And woe betide you if you didn't arrive promptly to collect your papers or did not have the correct money with you!

Hugh and John Neilson

The Neilsons, whose family built the present house at Drimsynie, lived in Corriesyke from 1932 to 1948, when it was sold to the Admiralty and became the Naval Base. They have some interesting memories of life in the village during those years.

One of the many characters in Lochgoilhead during the 1930s and 1940s was Major Methven, who lived at Drimsynie. Mainly through his own efforts he managed to produce a nine-hole golf course in front of the house and down as far as the road. (It was actually a twelve-hole course as three holes could be played from different tees.) Apparently the Major would use his old open-top Humber to pull a mower to cut the fairways, but being slightly the worse for wear he would often manage to mow some of the rhododendrons lining the drive up to the house and scare a few unsuspecting golfers at the same time.

Such was the Major's enthusiasm that in the summertime he would organise cricket matches between the villagers and the Boys' Brigade, who enjoyed summer camps at Lochgoilhead. He also organised clay-pigeon shoots and often arranged a match at New Year with a team from Inveraray.

During the war the Neilson boys and Major Methven's daughter, Georgina, were taught their lessons at Drimsynie by governesses, but Hugh doesn't remember learning very much.

Hugh Cameron-White

Until 1944 Hugh lived with his mother (his father was an officer in the Royal Navy) in a small house by the name of The Bungalow, which stood at the right-hand side at the top of the lane that runs between Daisy Bank and Primrose Bank. A Gaelic speaker himself, he remembers that there was still a lot of Gaelic spoken in the countryside round about. He was told by a man called John Tyre, who lived in Callander Cottage and worked for Glasgow Corporation Parks Department, that the name Hell's Glen came from a corruption of "iarann", the Gaelic for "iron", as at one time there were iron deposits in the glen; the Gaelic for "hell" is "ifrinn" or "iutharn".

9.8 The original golf course at Drimsynie; the figure nearest to the photographer is possibly Major Methven, and the caddie is James Henderson, Major Methven's gamekeeper

visitations from the minister, the Revd J. M. Campbell. He of course walked all the way there and back. Nicol MacNicol was also a shepherd. Duncan Campbell, formerly of Inveronich (another relative of Hugh's), remembered him singing Gaelic songs at the school in about 1910 at the command of the then headmaster, William Gilchrist.

Jessie MacNicol was the last of the family to leave Stuckbeg – she had lived there all alone for some years. She went to marry Archie Campbell, a

9.12 The MacNicol family outside Stuckbeg

gamekeeper on the Lithgow estate at Ormsary, on Loch Caolisport. Jessie was one of the last native speakers of "Lochgoil Gaelic", and in 1980 the School of Scottish Studies heard about her and sent a team to record her speaking about her childhood beside Loch Goil. Hugh, who also speaks Gaelic, used to visit her at Ormsary before her death in the mid-1980s, and they would talk of days gone by and sing a few Gaelic songs. He thinks her brother Nicol MacNicol was the last native speaker of all. He was a shepherd and died in Dunoon at an advanced age in the 1990s.

Hugh's grandmother, Annie Cameron, lived as a girl in Stuckiebeg, the cottage adjacent to the MacNicols. In the dark winter evenings, when they were walking home from school, their mother would be standing at the door waving a lantern to show them the way. After the Cameron family vacated Stuckiebeg, Coll Turner, a foxhunter, moved in. He was known locally as Old Coll the Foxhunter. He was found dead on 12 February 1913, at the age of 73, on a rustic bench between Stuckbeg and Lochgoilhead, his head resting on his backpack. He is buried in the churchyard, and his tombstone, near the church door, was raised by public subscription. The last tenants of Stuckiebeg, during the First World War, were Irish labourers, and the MacNicol children were warned not to go near because the house was allegedly infested with fleas!

***

LOCHGOILHEAD

by Hugh Cameron White, 1962

I dream of scenes of childhood as I watched the shepherd toil,
When the sun went down in evening o'er the village of Loch Goil,
Such scenes of rarest beauty there is naught for me can spoil,
As in dreams I dream of childhood and my home beside Loch Goil.

Now in memory I stroll once more the Glen Mor road I knew,
And I walk the banks of Donich where the pines obscure the view.
Or I stand there on Ben Bheula, why such scenes on earth are few,
As the evening sunshine taints with gold the village home I knew.

After schooltime in the summer, as we swam there by the pier,
How such happy scenes of childhood ring the bells of yesteryear.
And if one wish could be granted then that wish to me is clear,
'Tis my one desire to view once more my village home so dear.

Many friends have gone and left her, some are far beyond the sea,
And some lie in the churchyard resting 'neath an ancient tree.
But before I die, as die I will, my home once more will be
In that lovely peaceful haven of my village by the sea.

Bridget Jensen

Bridget grew up in Lochgoilhead in the 1940s and 1950s, before "modern" conveniences had arrived in the village. She lived at Ardroy.

Electricity came to the village some six years before it came round our side of the loch. We could look across at night and see the streetlamps. Our houses had been wired at the same time, but the supply wasn't on. Every now and then we would get a postcard telling us that the supplies would be cut off, perhaps for two hours on a Wednesday afternoon, "for essential repairs". That always raised a wry smile. But we did have our own gas supply, which every day involved my father winding up a huge circular weight on a pulley fixed high on the outside wall of the house. We had gaslights and a fridge. Eventually, when I was twelve, we got our power. I remember being quite frightened at first of switching on lights, and for some reason I disapproved of the new washing machine. "I suppose you'd prefer it if I was beating the clothes against stones in the burn", my mother said, exasperated.

I remember when the first bananas came to the village after the war. There was one banana to each child – rather pathetic pale fawn things, not at all like the ones we had seen in illustrations. My mother took my banana. Half of it she mashed with sugar and jam and cream and made a pile of sandwiches. The other half went to making banana ice cream in the gas fridge. All quite delicious, but I did feel she might have asked me first before sharing it all round!

About fifty years ago Lochgoilhead was completely snowed in for ten days or so. It was a magical time for us children. The school was closed, and the snow was that dry, squeaky kind which is perfect for sledging and snowfights. Adults weren't quite so happy, especially the shepherds, who were hard at work rescuing sheep from the huge drifts, and food supplies were beginning to run short. At last a small motor launch arrived from Arrochar, a man in the bows breaking the ice with a boathook. People gathered on the pier to welcome it. It had brought us newspapers, and Milanda bread from Glasgow, and paraffin for our lamps.

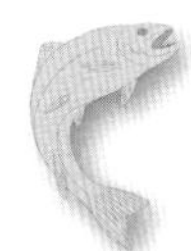

Chapter Ten

Clubs, Societies and Services

The Lochgoilhead Total Abstinence Society

The problems of drink and its excesses were as intractable in the late 1800s as they are today – or so it would seem from the necessity of calling a meeting on 8 February 1882 in the drill hall for the Total Abstainers of Lochgoilhead and Inhabitants. At the meeting, following the usual formalities of appointing an acting chairman, it was proposed that an association of total abstainers should be established, to be known as the Lochgoilhead Total Abstinence Society. Dr Burness was appointed as president, with Duncan Blair as junior vice-president, John McKellar as treasurer and James Blair as secretary. Other committee members were to include Messrs Neil Campbell, John Rae, Dugald McDugall, John MacLachlan, Duncan MacCallum and George M. Knox. Meetings were to be held throughout the winter on the first Tuesday of the month at 7.30 p.m. and by arrangement of the committee through the summer. Following the inaugural meeting, 61 men and 56 women were enrolled. Interestingly, several names (of 16 men and two women) were crossed out on the original minutes, though the reason is not stated; perhaps it was a failure to uphold the rules and moral standards of the society! The rules adopted by the committee were laid down for the approval of members, and were as follows:

1. *The object of the Society shall be the entire abolition of the drinking system.*
2. *The Society shall consist of all who shall sign and adhere to the following Bond of Union: "I agree neither to take nor give Intoxicating Liquors as beverages and to discountenance all the causes and practices of Intemperance".*
3. *That all members of the Society over or above fourteen(?) years of age pay one shilling each annually towards the maintenance of the Society.*

Lochgoilhead Scottish Country Dancing Club

The Scottish Country Dancing Club was started in 1950 in the old school by the two schoolteachers, Misses Stoddart and Leishman. In those days it is possible that dancers came closer to the society standard: Misses Stoddart and Leishman apparently taught their charges at the primary school to salute and curtsy to strangers to the village, so it is unlikely they would have tolerated the laxness that later pertained! Apart from locals the numbers were made up of forestry workers and engineers working on the Glen Shira hydroelectric scheme. Many of them brought their wives. Electricity had just reached the village, so four electricians who worked for Steve Gibson of Dunoon also attended regularly. At its peak the club had a membership of fifty. It has always maintained close links with the Dunoon club, whose members, for the past forty years, have returned for the annual end-of-season dance. For a couple of years in the early 1960s the club ceased to be, probably on account of the advent of television. However, it was soon resurrected, and it prospered under the leadership of Betty Cameron until she hung up her dancing shoes in 1991. The following poem was dedicated to Betty on her retirement:

As winter comes and the tourists depart,
It is time for our many clubs to start.
There's curling, bowling and art club too,
So many to mention, so much to do.

But the "pièce de resistance", no question at all,
Is our country dancing in the village hall,
Where for thirty-five years you have struggled in vain,
Hoping high standards one day we'd attain.

But you'll remember these times with fondness, we hope,
When with intricate moves we just could not cope –
With half-reels, corners, and turn, and cast,
With cries of "Jimmy! You're going too fast!"

When we pushed and we shoved to get back to our places,
With grim determination shown on our faces,
And when Belle had to remember "Am I lady or man?"
And when her lefts and her rights got the better of Nan.

10.7 The country dancers thank Belle Byrnes for her sterling years as a teacher, Christmas 2000 (back row, left to right): Eileen Cameron, Bill Cameron, Mike McCloghrie, Peter McNab, Revd James MacFarlane, Jack Wilson, Jean MacFarlane (face hidden), Cecilia Ferguson, Sadie MacKenzie, Julie Frize, Chris Hayes, Ann Birdsall, Emma Fuller, David Birdsall; (front row) Bernie Cullen, Eileen McCloghrie, Margaret Ferguson, Caroline Wilson, Jo Hardy, Belle, Elias Pagias, Bridget Jensen, Mary Buchanan, Jimmy Paterson (hands only)

As for Ronnie MacLeod, well, what can one say
About his nimble footwork as he danced a strathspey?
Society standard: well, it may never come,
But there's one thing for sure: we always have fun.

So thank you, Betty, from all of us here
For keeping us at it for many a year.
Enjoy your retirement and well-deserved rest.
Lots of luck, lots of happiness and 'orra best.

The club continued with around twenty regular members under the guidance of Betty's long-suffering successor, Belle Byrnes, until Christmas 2000, when she handed over to Julie Frize. Since Julie left the village in 2003 the club has been operating on a cooperative basis.

10.10 Members of the Fiddle Workshop with their tutor, Amy Geddes (left to right): Katherine Leyland, Thomas Ducat, Kevin Wykes, Mike McCloghrie, Pauline Divitt, Lynn Williams, Anne Goudie, Sandra Dickson, Evie Campbell

money and commercial sponsorship. It has added a great deal to the community life of the area by involving everyone, not just those interested in learning the fiddle. It has put on numerous concerts with such leading professional performers as Duncan Chisholm, Fine Friday, the Whistlebinkies, Amy Geddes and Sandy Wright, and Malinky, and even Jamie Laval, the USA Scottish Fiddle Champion from Seattle.

Loch Goil is now firmly on the traditional music map of Scotland, with enthusiastic audiences of up to 150 gathering for the concerts. Workshop members themselves have played at a number of local functions to help other clubs and organisations raise money, or just to add some music to their events. Even those who are not into traditional music get something out of the efforts of the workshop, as it has also organized arts, crafts and music weekends and author and storytelling events.

The workshop aims to restore music to the heart of the community, so that everyone can enjoy this fascinating part of the local heritage, whether they play or not.

The Local Newsletter

A local newsletter, the *Loch Goil Report*, was started in 2003 at the instigation of Mark Morpurgo, who felt that the unofficial village grapevine and the placing of notices in the shop windows could be improved upon as a method of telling people what is happening in the area. The support of local businesses who placed adverts has meant that the newsletter is available free of charge (though donations towards the costs of production are of course welcome!).

The *Goil Report* lists over 60 local enterprises and all the clubs and associations active in the area. By giving a full rundown of forthcoming events it enables residents to know what is going on in the village, and holiday-home owners and visitors can, if they wish, plan their visits to coincide with whatever interests them. By both previewing and reviewing events, the newsletter has helped increase attendance and promote the clubs that are active (more than 30 of them!), and puts people in touch with others who have similar interests. It also provides a communication vehicle for the Community Council and Community Trust to inform everyone what they have been up to and what their plans are for the future. There is a letters page for those prompted to put pen to paper, and there have been useful articles such as "Driving on single-track roads" by David Birdsall as well as profiles on the outdoor centres.

The Computer Club

The computer club was formed in September 2002 at the suggestion of Alex Burgess to allow people to get together and swap knowledge and ideas. The members meet fortnightly in the library of the village hall, some with laptops, and help each other understand the intricacies of computer software, from spreadsheets to production of illustrated calendars. They have also produced greetings cards for sale to raise funds for the church.

The National Park and Lochgoil Community Trust

Loch Goil and its surrounding area is part of the new Loch Lomond & the Trossachs National Park, set up in 2000, and Lochgoil was one of 24 communities in the park that received assistance from the park's Community Futures Programme. This was set up to prepare community action plans so that the park authority could better understand and work with the communities within its boundaries, and the Lochgoil plan was written after extensive consultation with residents. In addition, help was received from the park to establish the Lochgoil Community Trust, which came into being in January 2003 as a registered charity, principally in order to apply for funds that are unavailable to the community council. Apart from working alongside the council, the trust can initiate its own projects or cooperate with

Lochgoilhead Playgroup

In the mid-1970s a group of mothers felt the need to give their young children the opportunity to play together constructively and decided to form a mother and toddler group. This also provided the chance for the mothers to exchange ideas and chat socially. The group soon evolved into one of the first playgroups in Cowal and thrived, despite the description "Lazy Mothers' Club" given by some of the older, "traditional" members of the community. It proved to be very successful in developing the youngsters' social skills and giving them an appreciation of "working" and playing together in a sharing, caring atmosphere.

In the early years no funding was available and parents had to cover all the costs themselves. Coffee mornings and other fund-raising events kept the group active. This continued for a period of twenty years or so, until pre-school vouchers were introduced in 1998, when the playgroup attained nursery status. The resulting additional funds enabled the purchase of new equipment and better resources on a scale not previously available. The playgroup continues to thrive and will hopefully do so for many years to come.

The Scottish Holiday Camp and Club Pavilion

From May to August every year from 1903 the field between Inveronich and the River Goil housed the Scottish Holiday Camp, originally owned by the YMCA. The Club Pavilion, made mostly of iron and wood, was built by Cowieson & Co. of Glasgow in 1908 and consisted of a dining hall for 500 people, 26 bedrooms and 32 "cubicles", a reading and writing room, a dark room for amateur photographers, bathrooms (with hot and cold water), an office, stores, and "abundant lavatory accommodation on the most approved principles". In addition there was a ladies' room for the convenience of visitors and picnic parties and a store for cycles. The building was lighted with gas. Concerts were held weekly in the dining room, which was also used in wet weather for recreation; there was a piano and indoor games were provided. Outdoor accommodation consisted of bell tents fitted with wooden floors. Some had iron bedsteads, and all had mattresses, pillows, sheets and blankets.

The camp had its own motorboat, the *Ardgoil*, presented by the honorary vice-president, Mr Cameron Corbett (who had gifted the entire Ardgoil peninsula to Glasgow Corporation). It could carry 20 passengers and made weekly excursions to Arrochar, Loch Lomond and Loch Katrine and was also

10.16 The club pavilion of the Scottish Holiday Camp, 1911

used to meet parties coming to the camp via Whistlefield and Portincaple. Every year there was a sports day, which was very well supported, with a special prize given to the competitor who gained the largest number of points. There were also prizes for the best set of photographs of the camp or camp sports, landscapes, sports views and postcards. An exhibition of the photographs sent in for the competition was held at the YMCA headquarters at Bothwell Street, Glasgow.

Camp prices in 1911 were £1 per week for a tent (1/- extra for an iron bedstead), 22/- for a cubicle and 24/- for a bedroom. Visitors could be invited to join the regular meals, priced at 1/- for dinner and meat tea and *6d.* for plain tea and supper. Campers were expected to wear a camp badge (price *3d.*) fastened to their left coat lapel to help identify and assist one another. Photography materials were available at the camp shop. Refreshments could be purchased from the buffet at any time on week days, and campers going out for the day were provided with sandwiches free of charge. There were, however, strict camp rules:

1. *Only young men of good moral character are eligible for admission to the Holiday Camp, and should anyone prove by word or deed to be otherwise, he will be instantly expelled.*
2. *The use of intoxicants, gambling and improper language is strictly prohibited.*

10.17 Inside the dining hall of the club pavilion, 1911

3. *On week nights lights out at 11.00 p.m., Sundays 10.30 p.m.*
4. *A sentry patrols the camp at night. It is his duty to report any campers who, by talking, laughing, singing, or in any other way, disturb their fellow campers between 11.30 p.m. and 6.30 a.m.*

From the comments in the visitors' book it seems that the rules were not considered too onerous. "F. G." of Glasgow wrote: "This has certainly been the best holiday I have ever spent. I find the good influences at work here are calculated to enable a young man to go back to his everyday life in every way better fit to play the man"; "R. N." of London remarked: "Most spanking holiday ever had, will come again"; and "P. M. D." of South Shields observed: "I came to Lochgoilhead and found perfection. Perfect scenery, a perfect camp, perfect management, and perfect companionship."

The camp was bought in the 1940s by Glasgow Corporation. During the war years the Pavilion was known as Mossbank and was used temporarily as an approved school for young male offenders. Unsurprisingly this was not particularly popular with the locals, especially when it was perceived that their presence coincided with several incidents of housebreaking. After the war the camp was used to enable Glasgow schoolchildren, who might otherwise never have had the opportunity of a holiday, to take a rare break away from the city. They arrived via steamer and made their way by foot from the pier while their luggage was transported by pony and cart. Dances were held most weekends to which local children were invited.

10.18 The YMCA camp, seen looking up towards Pole Farm; Donich Lodge is in the foreground

***

LOST ON MOUNTAINS
THRILLS IN ARGYLL

A party of six holiday-makers, who had set out in the early evening from the YMCA camp at Inveronich, Lochgoilhead, Argyllshire, to climb Ben Donich, which is about 3000 feet high, had an alarming experience on the mountain. Losing their bearings, the party became split up, and, although four were guided back to the camp about 10 p.m., it was not until early the following morning that the others, a girl and a young man, were located and brought to safety.

When the four members returned without knowledge of the whereabouts of the other two, Mr David MacLachlan, a native of Lochgoilhead, and an experienced mountaineer, volunteered to make a search. All alone, he skirted the huge hill known as the Steeple, descended into the bed of the Donich Burn, in which he had to wade, and began the perilous ascent of the mountain in the darkness.

Nearing the summit, he heard cries far down the Glen Croe side of the Ben; and, led by these, and aided by the faint light of an electric torch, he managed to locate the wanderers – the girl weeping and wailing in a clump of bushes and the boy farther down towards the burn. Mr MacLachlan guided them home, the girl having to be partly supported and partly carried the whole way.

***

As the need for facilities such as the holiday camp decreased, the fabric of the building deteriorated, and in the 1960s, after years of neglect, it had to be knocked down.

The Lochgoilhead Centre

In 1964 Captain George Pound, a retired naval officer, and his wife, Biddy, bought Inverlounin in Lochgoilhead. The following year Scouts and Guides began visiting Inverlounin to learn to sail. There were two large huts at the bottom of the garden used for living and cooking facilities which could accommodate approximately 20 Scouts, and three or four old caravans were used by the Guides. It is also said that Captain Pound called on his friends to help, and that a minesweeper sailed up the loch to help lay a large jetty at Inverlounin. Soon the demand outgrew the space and other facilities were sought. The Forestry Commission owned the site in the village known as the Shelter Park, and the Scout Association began renting this in 1968 before eventually buying it.

The Forestry Commission left behind a few basic huts, and these were used as living quarters. Boating continued from Inverlounin, with the youngsters being transported in an old orange minibus, until the early 1970s. During this time a great deal of voluntary work was carried out renovating the original structures left on site. What Captain Pound had initiated was to become the Scout National Activity Centre. In 1981 construction on a new accommodation and dining block began. This provided beds for 100 people and a large dining room with eight individual kitchen areas. Two staff bungalows were added in 1984 to replace the warden's and staff caravans. The centre was supported then, as now, by a large number of volunteers, and in 1992, after a massive amount of fund-raising, Cranstoun House was built. This provided accommodation and cooking facilities for volunteers; it now houses professional and trainee instructors who work at the centre.

To move with the times and meet the needs of its diverse clientele, in 1995 the centre ceased to be self-catering and began to provide meals. The main accommodation was upgraded in 1998 to form more flexible living spaces, and four new lodges along with a new office building were constructed. This was made possible through various funding bodies, including the National Lottery. Always keen to modernise, and putting safety first, the centre obtained its licence to run new adventurous activities, and following the Scouting Initiative made the centre more user-friendly for people with special needs. The year 2002 saw more construction with the addition of an activities building housing a workshop, an equipment store and new laundry facilities.

The centre is well used by Scout groups from throughout the UK and beyond, but has expanded its user-group portfolio and is now also extremely popular with schools, other youth organisations and special needs groups. It runs a wide and varied programme of both land- and water-based activities and offers training for many nationally recognised outdoor certificates up to instructor level. In 2005 the centre celebrates 40 years of providing a safe and fun environment for young people to experience the outdoors.

Ardroy Outdoor Education Centre

Ardroy Outdoor Education Centre was opened by Fife County Council on 23 June 1970 to enable young people from the county of Fife to receive as broad an educational experience as possible in their secondary-school years. Students were offered opportunities for sailing, rock climbing, camping, orienteering, canoeing, pony-trekking, hill walking and other similar pursuits (with all equipment provided), as well as to take part in environmental studies. When the centre opened the charge per pupil per day was 5/-, though children from counties other than Fife had to pay £2 per day.

In 1990, due to financial pressure within the education department at Fife Council, Ardroy was scheduled to close, but the following year the centre's management was taken over by Community Education and its outlook from his previous home in Tighnabruaich allegedly to escape the clutches of a wealthy widow who had fallen for him. The experience may have been a traumatic one, as he never married! However, according to his niece Gladys M. Shearer, the real reason he did not marry was probably because the woman he loved (his brother-in-law's sister) said she could not leave her parents. His death, in 1931 at the age of 61, was a result of visiting a patient while he himself was suffering from the flu, and afterwards he contracted pneumonia. Just before he died someone – "possibly Lady X" – sent him flowers, including white lilies (the funereal kind). He was mad, and said, "She might have waited till I was dead!" After he died his two sisters (who idolized him) moved to Battery Point.

Doctor Shearer was probably succeeded by Andrew Picken, who was the doctor in 1933 when the residents of Carrick were demanding that the road be built.

Dr Stalker retired to Lochgoilhead in the late 1930s at a very young age, having for personal reasons given up a practice in the Paisley area. Originally from Ardentinny, she remained in Lochgoil until her death. She lived at Drynan in Inverlounin Road, now known as The Peel House. On occasions she acted as locum for Dr Iain MacIntyre. She was very proud of the local babies whom she helped bring into the world, so much so that after her death each of these "babies" was left a small legacy in her will. She also bequeathed small legacies to some of the local people whom she felt had contributed in a beneficial way to village life. One such person was Jock Paige, who for over twenty years had voluntarily taught the local children to swim.

10.20 Dr Shearer outside The Cottage, 1920s

Dr Iain MacIntyre, the son of John MacIntyre, who was in post during the war years and trained people to carry out first aid, held his surgery at The Cottage until the mid-1970s. He had no waiting room, so patients had to shuffle about on the gravel outside, suffering the rain or the midges, until someone came out. He had a very large cupboard in his room stacked full of pharmaceutical samples, and after hearing what the problem was he would get out one of the samples and say "We might try this." As a result, of course, there were no repeat prescriptions, but no one seemed to suffer from this casual treatment! Many a time that Dr MacIntyre came home through Hell's Glen he would find a deer that had "fallen" and which subsequently went into the back of his car.

Dr Holmes inherited the practice from Dr MacIntyre, and between 1984 and 1988 he was joined by Dr Alistair Findlay. Dr Bob Kilpatrick arrived in Lochgoilhead in July 1988 and enjoyed the transfer of the surgery to the brand new health centre that was opened in 1999. His successor in 2003 was Dr Peter Joiner, who spent only a short period in the village. After a few months when the population was served by locums, Dr Peter Von Kaehne was welcomed in November 2004.

The new health centre meant that in 2002 a dental service started up one day a week, with dentists travelling from the Lorne Street practice in Lochgilphead. And in June 2004 the village gained a monthly travelling optician's service, provided by T & L Optical.

Postal Services

The current post office building was constructed early in the twentieth century for Mrs Haggart (the great-grandmother of Lochgoilhead's current postmaster, Rod Phillips), who ran the post office from 1908 to 1946. The manual telephone exchange was also housed there, and there was a small soundproof booth which enabled the postmistress to accept and send telegrams in confidence. The office was manned twenty-four hours a day and the night duty operator could snatch a little rest on a small camp bed until disturbed by the bell heralding an incoming telegram, or possibly a telephone call. Incoming telegrams had to be hand-written, and there was a steady flow of them. It was not unusual on the occasion of a wedding to have to accept around a hundred telegrams of congratulation. The postmistress or her assistant delivered the telegrams by bicycle, and sometimes when business was brisk locals would be employed as well.

10.23 Dougie Cameron in his fire chief's uniform, holding the certificate awarded him on the occasion of his retirement

in charge when the unit moved to its first custom-built fire garage.

The original fire equipment (of which two AFS-type helmets, an axe and belt, and a canvas portable dam remain in the village) was stored at Ian MacCallum's yard at the rear of the Scout Centre, but it was moved in 1950 to a fire box adjacent to a garage at the Lochgoilhead Hotel. In 1989 the unit was provided with a small wooden shed at the entrance to the Scout Centre, and in 1992 the volunteers were issued with their first fire appliance, a Ford Transit Volunteer Support Vehicle, which was garaged in the steading adjoining The Cottage, leased from Douglas Campbell. With the new fire garage came the complete complement of fire-fighting equipment, personal protection for the crew, and a specifically designed volunteer fire-fighting vehicle.

Chapter Eleven
Carrick

The name of Carrick is first recorded in 1428, when a legal summons was served on Duncan Campbell of Lochawe at "le Carryk". The castle and fortifications, the earliest parts of which date from the late fourteenth century, were originally a Lamont stronghold, and are not mentioned until 1529. In that year, and in 1541, Archibald, fourth Earl of Argyll, granted it in liferent to successive countesses. A notarial document was executed by the fourth Earl of Argyll in 1540 in "the chapel of the Blessed Virgin Mary of Carrick in Lochgeillishead", which may refer to the oratory in the central upper chamber. It is said that the castle was "constantly used" as a safe store for the Campbell family charters: in 1641 the Marquess of Argyll gave instructions for "several writs" to be taken "out of our charter kists". The importance of the castle as a staging post between the Clyde and Loch Fyne is attested by the visit of Mary, Queen of Scots, in July 1563, when she was on her way to Inveraray.

Carrick Castle was held for the earls of Argyll from the late fifteenth century to 1685 by hereditary captains descended from the Campbells of Ardkinglas. The earliest of these was Robert Campbell, "constable of Carrick", whose name is first mentioned in 1494. A charter of 1672 by Archibald, ninth Earl of Argyll, to John Campbell specified the lands attached to the castle. These extended along the western shores of Loch Goil and Loch Long from Lettermay to Stronvochlan, near Ardentinny, and included a mill and the ferry of "Pontindornack", near Knap, as well as isolated properties near Ardentinny, in Glendaruel and in Rosneath. But the duty of "faithfully guarding our castle in peace and war" was attached to Carrick's central properties, "Innermuch" and "Ardnanyne" (Ardnahein). The captain was required to maintain the castle, including a barn for making malt, at his own expense. In a bond of 1674 John Campbell undertook "to make my actual residence and dwelling in the said Castle of Carrick alsoft as conveintlie I may", to perform the usual duties required, "especiallie the resaving and keeping of prisoners", and to employ a porter and two nightwatchmen.

Alan Paul was the last ferryman to carry people between Lochgoilhead, Carrick and Portincaple. He lived in Alt-Renan, a house which was south of Ardnahein and which is no longer there. On schooldays he would ferry the children of a shepherd living at Knap, a cottage between Carrick and Ardentinny, to the school at Ardentinny. If for some reason, for instance bad weather, he was unable to make the return journey the children had no alternative but to traipse the 4 miles along the coast on foot. Before the road to Lochgoilhead was built, Carrick residents who wanted to go to the village could either go by boat or walk to The Lodge, where a lift could be had. The stone benches upon which the would-be passengers sat are still to be seen at what were the original Lodge gates.

Carrick School

Following the Education Act of 1872, side schools were formed in cases where it was considered that children lived too far away from the local public school. Such a school was generally under the charge of a young unqualified teacher, often one who was intending to go on into training. The school at Carrick was formed under this system in 1894, and evidently was not always in the most suitable of premises, as is shown by the following extract from the teacher's log book:

1924, 11 March ***Director of Education's Report on this school***

This little school was visited on 30.1.24 when the 6 pupils on the Roll were all present. The teacher is earnest and painstaking and under her guidance the pupils are progressing although some of them are backward. It was arranged that the school should open at 9.30 a.m. in order to permit of time being available for Religious Instruction and Sewing.

Certain defects in the School equipment have now been made good but the schoolroom itself is separated by a thin wooden partition from a grocer's shop with the result that at times the children's attention is seriously distracted. There is no water in the school available for washing or drinking purposes.

By the 1930s there was a dedicated school building, but when maintenance was required the pupils were transferred to the church. This worked well enough except for when Mother Nature called: since the church was without a toilet the children had to climb over a wall to the field beyond. Such a move took place in 1934:

August 28th	*School reopened this morning at 10.a.m. in the Church Session House. Only three pupils present. Owing to the lock on the former school door being damaged we are unable to have desks etc, removed. Notified Education Authority and also Mr Blair, Lochgoilhead, to have lock repaired. Received supply of books for school and also cleaning materials. Had intimation that Peter MacPhail had passed his Qualifying Examination.*
August 30th	*Mr Blair, Lochgoilhead, came today to repair lock on school door. Notified Mr MacPhail, Ardnahein, to come and remove school furniture.*
August 31st	*School furniture moved to Church Session House where school is being held now. Only three pupils present all week.*

For the three years before records ceased in December 1941 the intake of new pupils was very volatile, rising that same year to a high of 19. This was due to young evacuees being schooled in Carrick as a stopgap, sometimes for just a few weeks until they returned to their families in Glasgow or Greenock. But in the 1940s, with the fabric of the building deteriorating and with only two pupils, the McPhails of Ardnahein Farm, the school finally closed. Since then Carrick children have attended Lochgoilhead School.

11.2 Carrick Castle, 1937; the school building is on the left

present rate of decline, as Mr. Macquisten, M.P. for Argyll, recently pointed out in the House, the village will soon be derelict.

To remedy matters and restore the once flourishing hamlet of Carrick to its rightful place on the map of Argyll, all that is required is a three-mile stretch of road from Carrick to Douglas Pier. As the foundations already exist, the cost of the work would be negligible. The County Engineer himself has estimated that it would not exceed £4000.

Council's Plea

The plea put forward by the Council for not executing the work is that there is no money for it.

This the inhabitants refuse any longer to accept. Even if it were true at the moment, it certainly was not true from August 1929 until October 1931, throughout which period the Council insisted on putting the argument forward. On 31st October 1931 it was officially reported that:

"Large grants have been intimated by the Ministry of Transport towards the cost of road improvement schemes in Argyll. The grants now to be given total £205,636". [indecipherable] *the Scottish Office that the offer made to the Cowal District Committee in August 1929, of an offer of 50 per cent of the cost of construction was not withdrawn until October 4th 1932.*

Trifling Cost

From August 1929 until October 1932, then, the County Council could have carried out the work at a maximum cost to itself of £2000 and at this small cost righted one of the gravest, long-standing injustices any community has ever been called upon to suffer.

In rates alone, according to the County Treasurer's own computation, these people, who for over 20 years have been paying an annual sum of £600, far from receiving any reciprocal benefits whatever, apart from education, have been for most of the time as effectively cut off from civilisation as the St. Kildans were in the Atlantic.

***

Of course even after the road was built, residents and visitors could not be sure of unhindered access. In January 1984, Peter and Dorothy Speight, of

11.4 The road to Carrick, late 19th century

Springburn Villa, held a twenty-first birthday party for their daughter Erica at Carrick Castle Hotel. A number of guests had arrived from far and wide and were enchanted by the first flakes of snow that began to fall shortly after they had gathered at the hotel on the Saturday evening. The party unfortunately had to proceed without the band that had been booked, as it was unable to get into the glen. The guests, however, decided to enjoy their enforced stay and spent the Sunday building snowmen and throwing snowballs at one another. By Monday, when the village remained totally cut off, the mood had changed: people became concerned about work commitments and urgent appointments. Garry Broadbent and Lochgoil Cruisers came to the rescue to permit their escape by sea. Another mercy mission to the village was reported in the *Daily Record* of 24 January, as Ian Kennedy, chef at the Lochgoilhead Hotel, had collapsed with a suspected stroke and had to be airlifted out by a Royal Navy helicopter. It was the following Wednesday afternoon before the roads were fully open to traffic.

In the 1930s and during the war years there was a community living in tents south of Ardnahein which came to be known as Chinatown. These were mainly permanent dwellings, and the occupants furnished them with such "luxuries" as tables, chairs and iron-framed bedsteads. They were a home

11.6 Carrick Castle, c1950s

Syne we maist fell in love wi' the midges.
When the weather broke doon, and was drizzly and cauld,
The young folk turned restless and snarled at the auld,
They girned at their mither: they 'greed and cast oot,
Their life was a wearisome burden, nae doubt.
We kept sayin' to them the storm'll blaw past,
And thankfu' were we when the sun shone at last.
The grummelin' stoppit, and mirth ta'en its place,
Wi' joy in each bosom and smiles on each face
We welcomed the heat, and the midges.